Kinship Worldview: Indigenous Authors Going Deeper with Holistic Education

Kinship Worldview: Indigenous Authors Going Deeper with Holistic Education

Paul Freedman
Four Arrows (Wahinkpe Topa)
aka Don Trent Jacobs

INFORMATION AGE PUBLISHING, INC.
Charlotte, NC • www.infoagepub.com

Library of Congress Cataloging-In-Publication Data

The CIP data for this book can be found on the Library of Congress website (loc.gov).

Paperback: 979-8-88730-665-0
Hardcover: 979-8-88730-666-7
E-Book: 979-8-88730-667-4

All proceeds from the sale of this book will be donated to nonprofit organizations dedicated to supporting indigenous causes and the *Holistic Education Review*.

Copyright © 2024 Information Age Publishing Inc.

All rights reserved. No part of this publication may be reproduced, stored in a retrieval system, or transmitted, in any form or by any means, electronic, mechanical, photocopying, microfilming, recording or otherwise, without written permission from the publisher.

Printed in the United States of America

CONTENTS

Introduction: Introducing the Collection: "Kinship Worldview: Indigenous Authors Going Deeper With Holistic Education" vii
Four Arrows (Wahinkpe Topa) aka Don Trent Jacobs

Forword: Welcome ix
Paul Freedman

Endorsements xi

1. **From a Much Deeper Place: 'Indigenous Worlding' as Next Step in Holistic Education** 1
   Four Arrows (Wahinkpe Topa) aka Don Trent Jacobs

2. **American Education from a Tribal Perspective** 7
   Greg Cajete

3. **An Indigenous Perspective on Modern Education** 13
   Ilarion (Kuuyux) Merculieff

4. **Aboriginal Pedagogy: Integrity in Academic and Cultural Practice** 19
   Tyson Yunkaporta

5. **Plurality, Equity and Meaning Making with Indigenous Knowledges** 29
   Deepa Srikantaiah, Brett Grant, & Shytance Wren

6. Lakota Epistemology as Holistic Being 37
   Ethleen Iron Cloud Two Dogs

7. How It Might Have Been 45
   Devona Lone Wolf

8. Embracing Sacredness in Education: Indigenous Psychology
   and the Seven Daily Walks 49
   Arthur W. Blume

9. It's in Our DNA! Holism as an Indigenous Worldview
   Approach to Happiness 57
   Frank Bracho

10. Proven Sustainable Teachings from Indigenous and Maroon
    Peoples: A Model for Holistic Educators 63
    Sox Sperry

11. Recovering the Spirit, Bone by Bone: Colonization and the
    Classroom 69
    Amba J. Sepie

12. I Live Here 75
    Shannon Kenny

13. Living Holistically: Practicing the Navajo
    Principles of *Hózhą́* and *K'é* 77
    Miranda Jensen Haskie

14. Learning to Walk Relationally and Live Métis 81
    Jennifer Markides

15. Learning From the "Least of These": Haraway's "Making
    Kin," Filipino Indigenous "Kapwa," and Other Holistic (and
    Subversive) Ways of Knowing 89
    S. Lily Mendoza

    Book Review: Indigenous Wisdom for Restoring Our World 97
    Vicki Zakrzewski

    Biographies 101

INTRODUCTION

INTRODUCING THE COLLECTION

"Kinship Worldview: Indigenous Authors Going Deeper With Holistic Education"

Four Arrows (Wahinkpe Topa) aka Don Trent Jacobs
Antioch University

Four Arrows introduces the chapters in this volume and provides context for the reader.

Keywords: indigenous peoples, holistic education, sacred interconnectedness, kinship worldview

I am grateful for the opportunity to put together this important collection of essays. Holistic educators have long understood that the traditional, kinship, pre-colonial (Indigenous) approach to teaching and learning is the original model for "holistic education"—a phrase popularized in the 1980s to counteract the mechanistic and fragmented approach to mainstream schooling.

Indigenous Peoples recognized the problem of western schooling long ago. In 1744, Virginia's governing commissioners offered to sponsor a number of young men from the nations of the Iroquois Confederacy so they could attend Williamsburg College. After a day's discussion, the Confederacy wrote back stating they had previous experience with their boys who attended such schools and explained that they came back "totally good for nothing" (Hopkins, 1898, p. 240). They then offered to take a dozen of the sons of Virginia to school, promising to instruct them so they could "make true men of them." They meant to assure optimal development of a young person's physical, emotional, moral, psychological, and spiritual attributes. Such education would emphasize respect, responsibility, and reciprocity on behalf of all human and non-human life. It realized spiritual life forces and the lessons to be learned from the trees, wind, rocks, animals, waters and stars. It understood the sacredness of children.

The chapters that follow offer testimony to the holism of original traditional Indigenous ways of teaching and learning. Each narrative describes an Indigenous orientation to holistic education that goes deeply into a sense of sacred interconnectedness with all life on Mother Earth. They reflect a "coherent worldview encompassing the processes of the world and how we humans find meaning in those processes" (Wildcat, 2001, p. 7). Each article begins with an abstract and ends with a biographical sketch of the authors that include: Greg Cajete, Ethleen Iron Cloud Two Dogs, Frank Bracho, Ilarion Merculieff, Jennifer Markides, Lily Mendoza, Devona Lone Wolf, Miranda Haskie, Sox Sperry, Tyson Yunkaporta, Amba Sepie, Shannon Kenny, Arthur Blume, Deepa Srikantaiah, Brett Grant, and Shytance Wren. We also have a featured book review of *Restoring the Kinship Worldview* by Vicki Zakrzewski and a republication of my chapter in the *International Handbook of Holistic Education* are also contributions to this special issue.

FORWORD

WELCOME

Paul Freedman
Salmonberry School, Eastsound, WA

Paul Freedman offers context and appreciation for this volume's collection of essays and their authors.

Keywords: Deep Learning, Holistic Education, Indigenous Knowing

Education, a field dedicated to nurturing human development towards optimal unfolding has drifted far from this ideal. I have committed my career to studying and doing my best to embody a model of teaching and learning that is holistic. There are ways of educating that instill deeper connections to self, to community and to nature. But at this time, as we are in the throes of the Anthropocene extinction, a time when we so desperately need to be cultivating these kinds of deep connections, even educators who appreciate this vision, often seem to be limited to atrophied gestures. We attempt to simply layer on reform efforts atop a narrowly defined, standards-based curriculum and methodology. It is not enough even to teach mindfulness, to meditate with our students, or to bring our classes out into nature. These are all welcome additions to modern schooling that have been espoused by holistic educators, but we must go deeper, to redesign education from a wholly different worldview.

Kinship Worldview: Indigenous Authors Going
Deeper with Holistic Education, pages ix–x.
Copyright © 2024 by Information Age Publishing
www.infoagepub.com
All rights of reproduction in any form reserved.

I am truly honored to bring forth this collection of essays and a poem from this diverse group of indigenous authors and scholars. This volume features some of the leading voices in this field. Individually, these voices articulate moving descriptions and powerful analyses from a range of indigenous approaches to pedagogy. Collectively, these voices form a sacred chorus. One that sings of a path towards re-enchantment and reconnection with the cosmos. It is both challenging and inspiring to read and reflect upon the words contained here.

In my 2015 TEDx talk, I spoke about *depth* as the missing and needed metaphor in education. We educators are obsessed with racing across surfaces, "covering" curriculum, always seeming to favor breadth and eschewing opportunities to explore in depth. Where I live, on Orcas Island in the Salish Sea, the traditional home of Coast Salish people, modern boaters still use nautical charts, on which ocean depth is indicated by small numbers representing fathoms. The fathom is a standardized measurement of 6 feet, originally meant to approximate a human arm span, or in other words, the maximum capacity of an eco-sapien hug. We measure the sea's depth in hugs. The verb "to fathom" means to understand. Educating children and adults towards understanding, and hopefully towards wisdom, should be about integrating this word fathom's two meanings: the noun and the verb. Education should be the embrace of, new learning, old ways of knowing, and profound understanding, as we travel together, deeper and deeper on these learning journeys with our students.

Welcome, dear readers, to a prodigious gathering of indigenous authors, a colloquium of learned scholars. As my friend, colleague and co-Editor Four Arrows points out, these voices speak to a *deeper* way of living, a *deeper* way of knowing, and a *deeper way of educating*. Enjoy their words and let the chorus immerse you in its wisdom. I invite you to consider the implications. Deeply.

And now, I will take the advice of Quuxut (Ilarion Merculieff) and "stop talking."

ENDORSEMENTS

This is an extraordinary collection of essays by wise Indigenous educators who share wisdom and practices from their personal experiences. In reading these, it becomes heartbreakingly clear how our profound levels of disconnection from each other and Mother Earth have brought us to this present reality of disaffected and lost students, exhausted teachers, overwhelmed administrators, and the escalating intrusion of political agendas into the classroom. Thankfully, for those of us willing to stay in the struggle, this beautiful work offers true solutions for how to reconnect with Life's energies and persevere together, just as Native peoples have done for millennia. I am so grateful for this book

—Margaret Wheatley
Author of 12 books from Leadership
and the New Science to Restoring Sanity

We two legged, big brained, hominid creatures are kin to all that ever was, is, and ever will be. The contributors here ask what that means for how we think, learn, and educate our young. This is no fringe pedagogy, but educational first responders coming to rescue a culture in a five-alarm crisis. It is a very good time

---

Kinship Worldview: Indigenous Authors Going Deeper with Holistic Education, pages xi–xiii.
Copyright © 2024 by Information Age Publishing
www.infoagepub.com
All rights of reproduction in any form reserved.

to reconsider education—the process of drawing forth—and summon the Angels of our better natures, who have been there all along.

—David W. Orr, Oberlin College emeritus;
Arizona State University, Professor of Practice,
Editor, Democracy in a Hotter Time *(MIT Press, 2023)*

For too long, we have sought to impose the tyranny of our pulverising mind on the self-creating, self-organising, and self-sustaining generosity of the all-blessing universal soul manifesting itself in all phenomena—unconditionally and impartially. Modern education, for all the good that it has done, has progressively alienated itself from the nourishing graces of the Sector Noble it was meant to be and stands in dire need of resuscitation and restoration to its original purpose. The present anthology offers, in my view, a most compelling invitation to look into the soul of education deriving its vital life-force from the deep recesses of the fecund womb of all-embracing sovereign Nature.

—*Thakur S Powdyel, former Minister of Education
Royal Government of Bhutan*

In my conversation with Four Arrows (2012) it became apparent that holistic educators can benefit greatly by listening to the voices of Indigenous educators. Holistic education can sometimes be too head centered and ignores body and spirit. The material in this book can help holistic educators deepen their work so that they can "walk their talk" more fully by connecting more directly to the Earth and Spirit.

—*Dr. John (Jack) Miller, Professor, Curriculum, Teaching and Learning,
The Ontario Institute for Studies in Education at the University of Toronto*

There was a time when human cultures shared a worldview that enabled them to recognize the sacred within themselves, within each other, and within the world around them. Disruptions to this worldview have resulted in a dominant culture that elevates human beings above Nature and other beings. This is the same worldview that justified dehumanizing people and wiping out entire cultures in the name of progress. Our children are being educated within a system birthed out of those values. This is a moment to pause and reclaim the wisdom of our ancestors in the form of indigenous worldviews and the invitation they offer to come back into right relationship with Nature and with each other.

In this collection of essays Four Arrows and his colleagues invite readers to engage with thoughtful commentaries about how to adopt an indigenous perspective on questions around the purpose and practice of education. Accompanied by pragmatic suggestions about what these values could mean in our engagement with children, communities and families, this volume is a reminder to each of us that the world we live in reflects our own understanding of what is possible and what is real. For those of us yearning for a shift from the status quo of dominant culture, these voices offer us a path forward.

—*Dr. Ulcca Joshi Hanson, Education Futurist and Author,*
The Future of Smart: How Our Education System
Needs to Change to Help All Young People Thrive

Four Arrows and his esteemed colleagues, present significant support and enthusiastic encouragement to educators towards strengthening the positive aspects of Holistic education and teaching, from an Indigenous perspective.

The use of the Oral Tradition is critical, use of storytelling, and teachings within Nature are the vehicles of learning from varied sources and input! Including the ways of learning for balance of body, mind, emotion, and spirit within the framework of interactive and cooperative society, reflect our great hope for the well being of our varied People's, the Mother Earth, and All Our Relations, unto the Seventh Generation ahead, with gratitude for the Seven Before. Excellently crafted, Megwiich Relatives!"

—*David D. West, MA, Director Emeritus*
Native American Programs, Southern Oregon University

For millennia holistic education was a natural way of being for indigenous peoples. They did not have to be "taught" about humanity's relationship to the web of life. They were an integral part of that web. In two words, Mitákuye Oyás'iŋ, the Lakota Sioux say "all my relations," a prayer of oneness and harmony with all forms of life. This collection of articles, *The Kinship Worldview* will touch your heart and open your eyes to a way of living this relationship for yourself and the learners in your sphere of influence.

—*Dr. Philip Snow Gang, Founder and*
Dean of The Institute for Educational Studies (TIES)

This profound collection of wisdom moves beyond just Indigenizing our worldview in education to truly embodying our relationship to Earth and Spirit. The voices presented offer the reader not just a way to decolonize our current western construct of relationships but a way of knowing and being in our interconnection to the more than human world. In this challenging worlding landscape we find ourselves in, our histories deep in our being rise up and call upon us as humans to (re/en)vison what education means when we learn from all sentient beings.

—*Dr. Marni Binder, Associate Professor Emeritus,*
School of Early Childhood Studies
Toronto Metropolitan University

CHAPTER 1

FROM A MUCH DEEPER PLACE

'Indigenous Worlding' as Next Step in Holistic Education

Four Arrows (Wahinkpe Topa) aka Don Trent Jacobs
Antioch University

This chapter introduces ways to deepen implementation and future research relating to a holistic education that can help us find ways to truly regain balance in our world. Because holistic education has largely been 'worlded' into dominant Eurocentric ways of being in the world, it calls for "Indigenous Worlding" as a way to restore the original Indigenous foundation for holistic education.

Holistic education, grounded in a fundamentally different worldview, reflects very different assumptions about education and school.
—*Ron Miller (1997, p. 5)*

Indigenous education embodies these principles more deeply ... When Indigenous people speak about our relationship to earth and the universe, it does not come from the head but from a much deeper place.
—*John (Jack) Miller (Four Arrows & Miller, 2012, p. 3)*

Jack Miller refers to holistic education as being about "holding a sense of the sacred, valuing the web of life, and educating the whole human being" (Four Arrows & Miller, 2012, p. 9). He writes elsewhere: "The holistic ideal can be traced back to Indigenous cultures. In general, the Aboriginal or Indigenous person sees the earth and the universe as infused with meaning and purpose and not as cold and impersonal as in the modern worldview" (Miller, 2009, p. 291). Miller's words reflect the recognition that Indigenous worldview is the ultimate foundation for holistic education. Unfortunately, holistic education has been held back by post-colonial worlding, defined as the result of colonizing hegemony being intrinsic to most educational systems in dominant cultural schooling. As a result, implementation of this holistic ideal has fallen short of what we need to achieve in education.

One way I feel holistic education does not go deep enough relates to degrees of anthropocentrism. I have noted that holistic education publications focus on body, mind, family, social community, art, pluralism, and health without an authentic and consistent engagement with the other-than-human relations. When "web of life" concepts are mentioned, authors seem limited by hegemonic assumptions relating to financial and technological considerations for human benefit. Kopnina (2014) critiques this problem, writing, "Mainstream neoliberal discourse tends to maintain instrumental and essentially anthropocentric attitudes toward environment, subordinating 'natural resources' to economic and social objectives" (p. 6).

However, even Kopnina's critical pedagogy does not go deep enough. His scholarship sees anthropocentrism as ethically wrong and a bad way to do environmental work, but it does not understand how other-than-humans offer solutions as sentient beings. It misses the spiritual interconnectedness dimension (Jacobs, 1997). O'Sullivan (2005) complains about this when he writes, "My major criticism of critical pedagogy is the pre-eminent emphasis on inter-human problems frequently to the detriment of the relations of humans to the wider biotic community and the natural world" (p. 411). Gustauo et al. (2005) are equally explicit about this problem when they say that critical pedagogy-oriented interventions into Indigenous cultures often lack a deep understanding of their nature-based, holistic worldview.

Although a number of holistic educators tend to have a human-centered perspective, others come closer to the nature-centered Indigenous worldview on this. I have wondered if embracing Indigeneity is a reason why it seems that there are relatively few holistic education programs being implemented in the world. I could not find statistics to verify this assumption, but I did call Jerry Mintz, long-time director of the Alternative Education Resource Organization, to find out. I asked him how many alternative schools actually do holistic education. After a long description of statistics, he concluded: "I might say that maybe 5–10% could be called holistic." An extensive study on interdisciplinary research in higher education (Van Noorden, 2015, p. 306) shows a similar lack of integrated or holistic perspective when he writes that, worldwide, 9–13% of all the scholarly publications reviewed showed any reference to a journal outside of the particular field of study targeted. Interdisciplinary curriculum is an aspect of holistic education because it encourages students to make connections between disciplines.

Thus, I contend that to move holistic education to its intended "deeper" orientation, we must return to our original non-anthropocentric worldview and begin to think and speak accordingly in the classroom. This would be a primary way to reworld Indigeneity into holistic education. Mika (2017), a senior lecturer at the University of Waikato and author of a new book on Indigenous metaphysics and "worlding," also refers to the unfulfilled Indigenous realization of holistic education rhetoric. Mika is supportive of holistic education as a twenty-first-century paradigm, and he pushes it further toward the deeper goals expressed in the opening quotes using Indigenous Nature-centered perspectives.

Mika (2017) goes deeper with his own description:

> Broadly I mean by *worlding* and its variations *worlded* and *worldedness* the following: one thing is never alone, and all things actively construct and compose it. As one thing presents itself to me others within it may appear and hide, but even if I cannot perceive them (which I cannot) we can be assured that they are there. An object that I perceive is therefore fundamentally unknowable. I can speculate on it and give it a name, but all I can be certain of is that it is mysterious precisely because it is 'worlded.' (pp. 6–7)

Such worlding requires that we incorporate worldview reflection into our holistic education classrooms. We must investigate the wisdom of our dominant worldview and its human-superiority assumptions to determine where and how it may impede the optimal utilization of holistic education.

This is something that Greg Cajete, John Lee, and I did in looking at how the dominant worldview lens guides neuroscientific conclusions. We discovered that the dominant worldview deters even neuroscientists from realizing the truths of Indigenous wisdom via their "observations" and interpretations of laboratory experiments (Four Arrows et al., 2010). Looking at fundamental Indigenous worldview beliefs, we found that much of Western science comes to faulty conclusions by looking at experiments through the Western lens. Such is the power of a worldview and why this worldview reflection is crucial for our holistic understanding of how we have managed to be on the verge of a mass extinction.

Although I continue to use it, the original word, 'worldview,' which comes from the German word "*Weltanschauung*" ("to see the world"), does not accurately describe the Indigenous worldview. It does not rely upon an understanding of the world by only what it can see. However, though 'worldview' does not align well with Indigenous ways of comprehending reality, it still works if we use it to explain fundamental ways we understand our place in the cosmos. It incorporates cultures, religions, and philosophies.

The concept of worldview may appear to be similar or even interchangeable with concepts such as ideology, paradigm, religion, and discourse, and they indeed possess some degree of referential overlap. However, worldviews can nonetheless be clearly distinguished from these concepts. (Hedlund-de Witt, 2013, p. 19)

Robert Redfield, the first social anthropologist and a specialist in worldview studies at the University of Chicago in the 1950s, also believed that worldview describes the totality of ideas that people within a culture share about self, human society, and natural and spiritual worlds (Redfield, 1953). He considered that since the Asian worldview had been mostly taken over by the Western one, that there remain only two worldviews for us to study—the primal or Indigenous one and the dominant one that continues to overshadow and destroy the original one.

With these ideas about worldview in mind, I believe going deeper with holistic education starts with seeking to find complementarity and understanding imbalances between the two worldviews. Then, with new awareness, educators must begin *worlding* the Indigenous perspective. We do this by actually participating in the world emotionally, physically, mentally, and spiritually, as if we are mysteriously inseparable from it and obligated to take action according to our highest potential for complementarity. It is a way of being in the world where distinctions between self and other disappear. I think of this as living fearlessly and, in so doing, embracing the full force of all things. By living the Indigenous worldview again, we cannot help but teach holistically.

REFERENCES

Four Arrows, Cajete, G., & Lee, J. (2010). *Critical neurophilosophy and Indigenous wisdom*. Sense.

Four Arrows, & Miller, J. P. (2012). To name the world: A dialogue about holistic and Indigenous education. *Encounter: Education for Meaning and Social Justice, 25*(3), 14–21.

Hedlund-de Witt, A. (2013). *Worldviews and the transformation to sustainable societies*. Doctoral diss. Vrije Universiteit Amsterdam. Dare.ubvu.vu.nl/bitstream/handle/1871/48104/dissertation.pdf

Jacobs, D. T. (1997). *Critical pedagogy and spiritual dialogue: The missing partnership*. Paper presented at Pedagogy of the Oppressed Conference. Omaha, NB: University of Nebraska.

Kopnina, H. (2014). Neoliberalism, pluralism, environment and education for sustainability. *Horizons of Holistic Education, 1*, 93–113.

Mika, C. (2017). *Indigenous education and the metaphysics of presence: A worlded philosophy*. Routledge.

Miller, J. P. (2009). Holistic education: Learning for an interconnected world. In R. V. Farrell & G. Papagiannis (Eds.), *Education for sustainability Volume 1,* (pp. 145–159). Encyclopedia of Life Support Systems, UNESCO.

Miller, R. (1997, 2016). *What are schools for? Holistic education in American culture* (3rd ed.). Alternative Education Resource Organization.

O'Sullivan, E. (2005). Education and the dilemmas of modernism: Toward an ecozoic vision. In D. E. Purpel, & H. S. Shapiro (Eds.), *Critical social issues in American education* (pp. 55–57). Lawrence Erlbaum.

Redfield, R. (1953). *The primitive world and its transformations.* Cornell University Press.

Van Noorden, R. (2015). Interdisciplinary research by the numbers. *Nature, 525*(7569), 306–307.

CHAPTER 2

AMERICAN EDUCATION FROM A TRIBAL PERSPECTIVE

Greg Cajete
University of New Mexico

In this chapter, Dr. Cajete offers the holistic context in which Indigenous-based learning exists. He contrasts this method with the relatively disconnected approach typical in American educational approaches. He calls for Indian voices to collaboratively bring forth a return to this holistic orientation, closing with 24 elements which characterize Indigenous education processes.

Keywords: Tribal Education, Learning, Indigenous Teaching, Curriculum Development

Learning is always a creative act. We are continuously engaged in the art of making meaning and creating our world through the unique processes of human learning. Learning for humans is instinctual, continuous, and simultaneously, the most complex of our natural traits. Learning is also key to our ability to survive in the environments that we create and that create us.

Throughout history human societies have attempted to guide, facilitate, and even coerce the human instinct for learning toward socially defined ends. The complex of activities for "forming" human learning is what we call "education" today. To this end, human societies have evolved a multitude of educational forms to maintain their survival and as vehicles for expressing their unique cultural mythos. This cultural mythos also forms the foundation for each culture's "guiding vision," that is, a culture's story of itself and its perceived relationship to the world. In its guiding vision, a culture sets forth a set of "ideals" which guide and form the learning processes inherent in its educational systems. In turn, these ideals reflect what that culture values as the most important qualities, behaviors, and value structures to instill in its members. Generally, this set of values is predicated on those things it considers central to its survival.

Traditional American Indian education historically occurred in a holistic social context which developed a sense of the importance of each individual as a contributing member of the social group. Essentially, Tribally-contexed education worked at sustaining a life process. It was a process of education which unfolded through mutual, reciprocal relationships between one's social group and the natural world. This relationship involved all dimensions of one's being while providing both personal development and technical skills through *participation* in the life of the community. It was essentially an integrated expression of environmental education.

Understanding the depth of relationships and the significance of participation in all aspects of life are the keys to traditional American Indian education. "*Mitakuye Oyasin*" (we are all related) is a Lakota phrase which captures an essence of Tribal education because it reflects the understanding that our lives are truly and profoundly connected to other people and the physical world. Likewise, in Tribal education, knowledge is gained from first-hand experience in the world and then transmitted or explored through ritual, ceremony, art, and appropriate technology. Knowledge gained through these vehicles is then used in the context of everyday living. Education, in this context, becomes education for "life's sake." Education is, at its very essence, learning about life through participation and relationship to community, including not only people, but plants, animals, and the whole of Nature.

This ideal of education directly contrasts with the predominant orientation of American education which continues to emphasize "objective" content and experience detached from primary sources and community. This conditioning for being a marginal participant and perpetual observer, involved with only objective content, is a foundational element of the crisis of American education and the alienation of modern man from his own being and the natural world.

Traditional American Indian forms of education must be given serious consideration as conceptual wellsprings for the "new" kinds of educational thought capable of addressing the tremendous challenges of the 21st Century. Tribal education presents examples of models and universal foundations for the transformation of American education and the development of a "new" paradigm for curricula which will make a difference for "life's sake" in the world of 21st Century.

American Indians have struggled to adapt to an educational process that is not their own with its inherent social, political, and cultural baggage. Yet American Indian cultural forms of education contain seeds for new models of educating which can enliven American education, as well as allow American Indians to evolve contemporary expressions of education tied to their cultural roots.

For American Indians, a new "Circle" of education must begin which is founded on the roots of Tribal education and reflective of the needs, values, and socio/political issues as Indian people themselves perceive them.

Such a new circle must encompass the importance Indian people place on the continuance of their ancestral traditions; emphasize a respect for individual uniqueness in the diversity of expressions of spirituality; facilitate a strong and well-contexted understanding of history and culture; develop a strong sense of place and service to community; and forge a commitment to educational and social transformation which recognizes and further empowers the inherent strength of Indian people and their respective cultures.

To understand how to accomplish this, Indian people must begin to exploit all avenues of communication open to them and establish a reflective dialogue about a contemporary theory for Indian education that evolves from *them* and *their* collective experience. In the past, Indian education has been defined largely by non-Indian educators, politicians, and institutions through a huge volume of legislative acts at the state and federal levels, which for decades have entangled Indian leaders, educators, and whole communities in the morass of the federal government's social/political bureaucracy.

Indeed, Indian education stems more from the U.S. Government's self-serving political/bureaucratic relationship with Indian tribes than any truly culturally-contexed process rooted in Tribal philosophies and social values. In fact, no contemporary theory of Indian education exists which can be said to guide the implementation or direction of educational curriculum development. Instead, what is called "Indian education" today is really a "compendium of models, methodologies and techniques gleaned from various sources in mainstream American education and adapted to American Indian circumstances, usually with the underlying aim of cultural assimilation" (Cajete, 2012, p. 41).

It is time for Indian people to define Indian education in their own voice and in their own terms. It is time for Indian people to allow themselves to explore and express the richness of their collective history in education. Among American Indians, education has always included a visionary expression of life. Education has been, and continues to be, a grand story, a search for meaning, an essential food for the soul.

BUILDING ON EARLIER REALITIES

The Mayan practice of building one pyramidal structure by encasing a pervious one provides an appropriate metaphor for the developmental building process of Indigenous education. At the end of each Mayan dynasty, the nobles of the reigning dynasty would commemorate their "new order" by erecting a symbolic new reality. In establishing this new reality, the nobles would engage in the building of a new ceremonial pyramid by encasing an older one. Thereby, encasing an older reality by building upon a new one. The new structure became the visible symbolic expression through which they espoused the new reality. As is evident from current excavations, these successive facades of "new reality" were actualized by recycling many of the materials used previously in the structures. A constant building upon earlier realities is really a basic Indigenous characteristic of process. The newest reality may seem different from earlier ones, but its essential essence and foundation remains tied to the earlier realities which it encases. The pyramids are restructured, enlarged, and remolded, but their ancient foundations remain.

Many of the temple pyramids served as tombs for the noble elite of each dynasty. The practice of burrowing into the heart of a pyramid to place a tomb metaphorically connected the deceased noble to the realities of both past and present. Building on the realities of past generations, expressing new realities with each dynasty while remaining true to basic principles and orientations, are reflective of the kind of structuring process to which the evolution of Indigenous education is naturally tied.

Extending the metaphor of the structuring of the Mayan pyramids to the "building" of a contemporary expression of Indigenous education, we have several images of structuring, of engineering the new reality built upon earlier ones, yet reflecting the needs and facing the sun of the times in which we now live. Education is always "in process" and essentially being built from the stones, and upon the foundations of, prior structures. Indigenous education has "prior structures," i.e., stones and foundations from which it can once again be built.

ELEMENTAL POINTS ABOUT INDIGENOUS EDUCATION

There are a number of elements which characterize Indigenous education and processes. These elements characterize the expression of Indigenous education wherever and however it has been expressed. These elements are like the "living stones," the "*Inyan*" as the Lakota term it, which animate the expressions of Indigenous education. A few of these characteristics are included here to provide "landmarks" to assist the reader.

- The sacred view of Nature permeates and contexts the foundational process of teaching and learning.
- Integration and interconnectedness are universal traits.
- Relationships between elements and knowledge bases radiate in concentric rings of process and structure.
- Rites symbolize various elements of its processes and structures.
- Its processes adhere to the principle of mutual reciprocity between humans and all other things.

- It recognizes and incorporates the cycles within cycles, i.e., that there are always deeper levels of meaning to be found in every learning/teaching process.
- It presents something to learn for everyone, at every stage of life.
- It recognizes the levels of maturity and readiness to learn in the developmental process of both males and females. This recognition is incorporated into the designs and situations in which Indigenous teaching takes place.
- It recognizes language as a sacred expression of breath and incorporates this orientation in all its foundations.
- It recognizes that each person and each culture contain the "seeds" of all that are essential to their well being and positive development.
- Art is used as both a vehicle of utility and expression. Art is recognized as an expression of the soul.
- It recognizes and applies ordering through ceremony, ritual, and community activity.
- The ritual complex is used as both structure and process for teaching key principles and values.
- It recognizes that the true sources of knowledge are to be found within the individual *and* entities of nature.
- It recognizes that true learning occurs through participation and honoring relationships in both the human and natural communities.
- It honors the ebb and flow of learning as it moves back and forth through individuals, community, nature, and the cosmos.
- It recognizes that learning requires letting go, growing, and re-integration at successively higher levels of understanding.
- Its purpose is to teach "a way of life."
- It occurs always within an authentic context of community and nature.
- It uses story as a way to root a perspective that unfolds through the special use of language.
- It recognizes the power of thought and language to create the worlds we live in.
- It creates "maps of the world" which assist us through our life's journey.
- It resonates and builds learning through the Tribal structures of the home and community.

These essential points are reflected in multiple ways through the contexts, methods, and expressions of Indigenous education. They can provide the building stones for new structures, new foundations, and new realities in contemporary Indian education. The key lies in our own collective ability to create the contexts in which they may most appropriately be applied in erecting a new expression of Indian education in a 21st century world.

REFERENCE

Cajete, G. (2012). Thoughts for American Indian education in a 21st-century world. In S. Mukhopadhyay & W.-M. Roth (Eds.), *Alternative forms of knowing (in) mathematics* (pp. 33–51). Brill Publishers.

CHAPTER 3

AN INDIGENOUS PERSPECTIVE ON MODERN EDUCATION

Ilarion (Kuuyux) Merculieff

Aluet Elder and Wisdom Keeper

Ilarion Merculieff offers a perspective on Indigenous worldview approaches to teaching and learning from his Unangan (Aleut) relatives and communities. He focuses on remembering that we are spirits inhabiting a body; that children must be treated as autonomous, sacred individuals; and that education must focus not on problems but on challenges that are opportunities for learning. He emphasizes that we are living in a world where we have reversed the laws for living that emphasize mind over heart.

Yupik Elders in southwest Alaska call our dominant cultures "reverse societies" or the "inside out societies." They believe we have reversed all the laws for living. For example, we used to honor and respect Mother Earth by taking care of her. We used to honor the wisdom of Elders. There were no old folk homes that kept elders out of sight, out of mind. We used to honor sharing our wealth with everyone. We used to focus on the greater good of the community and not just self-gain. We used to emphasize processes and not goals. Perhaps the most salient reversal is that we used to listen to our hearts. We let our hearts tell our minds what to do. The ills we face in our world stem from such imbalanced ways of being in the world.

Kinship Worldview: Indigenous Authors Going
Deeper with Holistic Education, pages 13–17.
Copyright © 2024 by Information Age Publishing
www.infoagepub.com
All rights of reproduction in any form reserved.

I was raised by my Unangan (Aleut) parents and the people of my village on St. Paul Island in the middle of the Bering Sea, in a way that reflects the Yupik perspective. My mother taught me that we are spirit beings coming into human form. As spirit beings, we are formless. When we come into life, we will have the trials and tribulations and learning experiences of human beings. When we die, our spiritual selves or souls continue on.

Many Indigenous peoples see infants as especially sacred because they know that babies just came from the spirit world. Knowing in their human form, infants will be vulnerable and easily traumatized, they are treated with the highest degree of kindness and care. Adults never scold or spank a child. When children cry, they are attended to immediately. They are surrounded by a loving community. In Western society, and indeed much of the world, we do and say things that intentionally or unintentionally result in trauma for the child. I feel that most children in the world are traumatized at a very early age, and this results in a diminished human being.

When I was a child, I was raised by an entire village of people who understood that they must always be positive, think positive, and do positive things with and around children. Every day, from age 5 until about age 13, whenever I encountered an adult, they would affirm me, and say something positive, like "aang laakaiyaax, exumnakoxt tyin" (hello boy, you are good). This occurred every day with every adult I encountered. Even when I stole money from my "papa" (my grandfather), at age 9, and was discovered, I was not scolded. I had wanted to purchase a plastic airplane in the government-run store that was called a "canteen" at the time. I wanted it so badly that I stole the 20 dollars. This was a lot of money for my people at the time. It took some an entire year to earn that much money.

Nevertheless, I stole the money and bought the airplane. I turned around after I bought the plane, and there was my aunt standing right behind me. I thought, "Oh-oh, I am caught." She didn't say a word to me until I was outside of the building. Then, she said, in a very un-accusatory and non-judgmental way, "Larry, where did you get the money to buy that plane?" I knew I had to tell the truth, so I told her I stole the money from my Papa. She paused, and said: "What do you think you should do about that?" Reluctantly, I said that I should return the plane and get the money back and tell my papa I took the money. She said, "Maaxoon" ("OK"). So, after I returned the plane, she reached into her pocket and paid for the airplane. She rewarded me for my actions. I went to my papa and told him I stole it from him. His response surprised me. He said, "Exumnakoxt laakaiyaax" (Good boy!).

I understood later in life that my aunt and papa were teaching me important lessons. They taught me to focus, not on what you don't want to see in the world, but on what you do want to see. In other words, we can help create our reality. and that will become the reality. I never stole again for the rest of my life. What my aunt and my papa did was to create the space for me to learn rather than scold me. Nor did they use any authority to tell me what to learn or how to learn. They left it to me to develop my autonomous ability to learn from experience and reflection. Thus, in the Unangan way, I grew up watching and listening to learn rather than asking others to tell me. It is in this way that I was given the freedom to expand my ability to think critically without the dictates of any adult. I believe this kind of education is foundational to authentic holistic learning.

From the way I was treated by the adults, I also learned that everyone is on their own sacred path and that we never interfere with another's sacred path. We may offer the child what we know, but whether or not the child picks it up is his or her choice. Ultimately, what they become is not something a parent can control. I also learned by the way the adults talked with me; I never was talked "down" to. They treated me as they would any other adult. The only difference was that they recognized that I lacked experience in life, so the only time they would intervene in what I was doing was when I was putting myself or others in danger that I didn't recognize.

My people understood that as a spirit being in human form, I was as intelligent as anyone else. My people did not label anyone as slow, or stupid, or having any disorder. Everyone has some form of genius in them. It is when the children are indoctrinated to listen to adults and to external authority that they lose their genius and self-authority. I have talked with children in schools throughout my career, and I can see the light in their eyes until about the sixth grade, when most lose this light. In these classes, I would ask each student to write down all the negative things about themselves, then all the positive things. The results were always lopsided. They would find dozens of negative things about themselves, and very few positive things.

In Unangan Tunuu (the Aleut language), there is no word for "problem" and so we do not recognize any experience in life as being a problem. Rather we saw them as opportunities. This idea was ingrained in me. As I went through life, any difficulties I had I saw as challenges, not problems, so I was able to deal with any situation I encountered as lessons to be learned. When I got to high school, I was sent to a Bureau of Indian Affairs boarding school in Chemawa, Oregon, 5 miles north of Salem, 2,000 miles from home. I was 12 years old in the 10th grade at the time. We called it going to school without love because we were "air bussed" from our home, with no contact with our parents for the entire school year, and yet this was not a problem; it was only an opportunity to learn many things. When I graduated from the 12th grade, I was advised by my high school counselor to choose a small college to have a better chance of success. I saw this as a challenge, so I applied to the University of Washington with an enrollment of 34,000 students. It was the largest single campus in the Pacific Northwest. It took me four and a half years, but I graduated.

Shortly after I arrived at the university, I noted that it did not have many Native Americans attending. At age 18, I decided to go to the university president to tell him that this institution was in a state that had 22 Indian reservations, and that there were only 4 people, including myself, that identified themselves as Native

Americans at the university. Of course, I was not familiar with the proper procedures to get to the president, so I just walked into his outer office and told the secretary I wanted to see the president. To make a long story short, the president agreed to see me, and I told him what I observed. He made a decision on the spot. He told me, "Ok, you obviously feel strongly about this, so I want you to recruit Native American students to the university. We will pay you and provide you with a vehicle."

At that time, I didn't know how to drive in a city, but I said I would do it. This was not a problem for me, but an opportunity. At age 18, I became the first recruiter, counselor, and financial aid advisor for what became the Native American program at the University of Washington. Today it has its own department. As the director for a Native American program at a major university, I was asked to be a member of the National American Indian Education Advisory Board, which advised the federal government on Native American educational issues. I was the youngest member. All the other board members were tribal chiefs or held some top position at a university. I saw this as a challenge that I accepted.

During my early 30's, I was offered a job with the State of Alaska to be the director of business development. I had one staff member in the State Department of Commerce and Economic Development. I did not think that we were too small to guide small businesses in the state. This was a challenge, not a problem. After a year in the position, the Commissioner asked me to create a single department focused on economic development for the state. At that time, we had Forestry, Fishery, Mining, Tourism, and Business Development that acted separately from one another. I accepted the challenge, and we organized as the Economic Development arm of the state, and I became its first director. We were successful in becoming a unified department because I utilized traditional talking circle formats where all personnel contributed to how the new department would function. As a result, the governor asked me if I would accept the position of the Commissioner of the Department of Commerce and Economic Development, a state cabinet post. I served as the first Alaska Native commissioner for the last 2 years of the governor's term in office. I had never served in a public office before or headed up an entire department with 2,000 employees, but I did only because it was a challenge, not a problem.

If holistic education is about meeting the social, physical, emotional, academic, and spiritual aspects of a child, then I believe the traditional Indigenous worldview I have been describing is essential. How different schools would be if they modeled the idea that things we encounter in life are challenges and not problems. Such modeling allowed me to be very successful in whatever I chose to do in life. Holistic educators should not tell our children what to learn, how to learn, and define everything. Doing so, in effect, tells the child: "Do not depend on yourself to know what to do; listen to the authority."

In these critical times we are in, I wish for education to focus on the world we wish to see, without focusing on the problems and reacting, but rather viewing it as an opportunity to take on a new challenge. What we are doing instead is to focus on stopping things that we don't wish to see in the world, be it political corruption, wars, refugees, the violation of women, and ultimately the violation of Mother Earth. My Elders say that we are "energy beings" mentally, physically, and spiritually. When we put our energies into what we want to stop, it only adds to the power of what we are trying to stop. Of course, we should act to stop the negatives in the world, but we should not put all our energies into that. For example, we have been trying to stop wars for a long time, but wars continue, and the world is experiencing increasing violence. There are thousands of more environmental groups trying to "save" the planet than there were 30 years ago, and yet today we have brought ourselves to the brink of extinction. We talk about equality but continue rigid hierarchies and discrimination.

We must focus on the world we wish to see with a worldview that recognizes our interconnectedness and that understands our spiritual journey on this wondrous planet. Otherwise, our children are being given a world that is bringing human beings to the precipice of near extinction for the first time in known history. The children are seeking answers, but they are not well equipped to think critically and "outside the box" for the answers. I feel that in order to raise children who are self-empowered and equipped to think critically in addressing the world's ills, we must listen to Indigenous peoples of the world who still remember what the old ways are telling us. In order for us to achieve peace and harmony in the world, we must become the things we wish to see. If we want peace, we must be peace; if we want love in the world, we must become love. We cannot work for peace when we don't have peace in ourselves; we cannot work for harmony on Mother Earth when we don't have harmony within ourselves. Nothing is created outside till it's created inside first. If we really want our children to be successful in life, we must focus on healing ourselves. The Indigenous Elders say that that is the most unselfish thing we can do for the world at this time of daunting challenges.

From the Unangan way, I learned to focus on affirming the positive, recognize and value my own experiences in life and those of others, to recognize and honor the spirit in human form, to think critically, and to have reverence for all in Creation. As educators who love children, we all can help instill these qualities in them.

CHAPTER 4

ABORIGINAL PEDAGOGY

Integrity in Academic and Cultural Practice

Tyson Yunkaporta
Deakin University, Melbourne, AU

Dr. Yunkaporta offers a possibility for all teachers to reach for holistic education's full potential. His analysis is specific to his unique Australian Aboriginal culture in a world of diverse cultures. He suggests, however, that it may be useful as a basis for inquiry for all educators, especially allowing Indigenous teachers, scholars, and community members to express abstract ideas about customary processes they have previously been unable to articulate in English. This empowering process can result in a way to liberate Indigenous teachers and learners, and others, from the colonizing heuristics of settler scholarship.

Keywords: Decolonizing Education, Aboriginal Pedagogy, Indigeneity, Education Theories

THE STATUS OF INDIGENOUS PEDAGOGIES

Aboriginal pedagogy, while enjoying brief periods of buzz-word status to add some spice to policy and syllabus documents, has struggled to find a place in the academy as a serious research topic, both in Australia (Hughes & More, 2004) and internationally (Battiste, 2002). It has been misaligned with the pseudo-science of Learning Styles Theory, which was debunked decades ago (Curry, 1990) but persists in the mythologies of progressive education.

Unfortunately, the 'woo-woo' factor of native wisdom has attracted the laziest scholars and practitioners, who like to throw Indigenous Knowledge into their basket of 'alternative' education theories like Learning Styles Theory, as a fig leaf for their indolence and a vehicle for their intellectual and cultural bypass.

While some common features of Aboriginal pedagogy that align with Western pedagogies have been acknowledged, such as place-based (Marker, 2006) and narrative pedagogies (Egan, 1998), it has been largely dismissed in the academy, while paradoxically being embraced by education institutions as a tokenistic, exotic add-on in curriculum (e.g., Yunkaporta, 2010). The topic is occasionally revived when it is found that customary Indigenous practices of knowledge transmission and production align with aspects of 'hard science' such as Neuroscience (Yunkaporta et al., 2020). However, I am only aware of one large-scale empirical study ever having been conducted, which was commissioned by an Australian government agency, and I am unable to reference this as I had to sign an NDA before viewing it.

In the global south, many of us find ourselves sublimating our traditional processes of knowledge transmission through compulsory engagement with the education institutions of the Anglosphere. Our customary learning practices are misaligned with the cognitive orientation favored in Western schooling, which tends to be individualistic and reductionist, isolating variables from the contexts in which they are used as well as from other interconnected variables (Bender & Beller, 2016). Students are prepared to become industrial workers who focus only on the work to be done, rather than the purpose and context for which that work is important, and even in the sciences variables tend to be isolated (Denny, 1983). There is an overwhelming focus on print literacy as a method of knowledge production that allows ideas and even words themselves to exist in isolation (Havelock, 1982).

MISMATCHED COGNITIONS

Schooling fosters an independent orientation that gives rise to analytic cognition characterised by taxonomic and rule-based categorization, a narrow focus in visual attention, dispositional bias in causal attribution and use of formal logic in reasoning (Varnum et al., 2010). This field-independent reasoning is often at odds with the customary cognitive practices of Indigenous people, which have been described variously as high context (Samovar & Porter, 2004), field dependent (Murdoch, 1988) or as distributed cognition (Arnau et al., 2013). An example of how this impacts perception in learning contexts is that students with an independent orientation will attend focal objects in visual scenes first, while students with an interdependent orientation will attend to the background first (Rhode et al., 2016). The former tends to sequence events and objects from left to right, while the latter sequence from east to west in alignment with solar movement, so may only exhibit a left-to-right orientation while facing south (Evans, 2009). This orientation has implications for teaching print literacy in Indigenous communities failing to comply with, or actively resisting, industrial development and schooling.

Adaptive, complex, and constantly evolving cognitive practices in oral cultures are characterised in structure and protocol by revolving feedback loops that are navigated, negotiated, and understood collectively (Murdoch, 1988). The logic cycle of those loops is reflected even in the grammar of Australian Aboriginal languages, for example, in the frequent use of negated antonyms (Sayers, 1976).

Language structure has been found to be an indicator of field-dependent cognition in many cultures, for example, in Korea, where background information precedes the subject and is usually placed at the beginning of a sentence to establish context (Rhode et al., 2016). It is misleading however to binarize Indigenous and non-Indigenous cognition arbitrarily as high or low context, considering the variance within communities as well as the fact that distributed cognition is not limited to Indigenous cultures. Indeed, it has been found in Scottish communities and other non-Aboriginal groups around the world (Murdoch, 1988), including many Russian communities in which the common variables do not include biology or Indigenousness.

One common variable is child-rearing practice that involves multiple carers, breast-feeding on demand, constant body contact, in-arms time, presence in adult activities with high levels of sensory motor stimulation, non-restrictive clothing and equipment, and no set routines for feeding, sleeping and toilet (Iliev & Ojalehto, 2015). This reflects customary and contemporary child-rearing practices in Australian Aboriginal communities (Martin, 1993).

Another variable in the retention of field-dependent cognition is the degree to which a culture has managed to avoid in recent centuries the intervention of the Catholic Church in the restructuring of families and communities to better facilitate wealth extraction from individuals, and the subsequent Protestant innovation of religious learning as an individualistic endeavor. This restructuring of societies to transition from collective to individual orientations (reducing relational ways of knowing) was further enabled by print literacy, which physically rewires the human brain in catastrophic ways (Henrich et al., 2010). Individuals entirely inhabiting this culture of occupation are not bound by the same community obligations, orientations and protocols that characterize the knowledge production and transmission practices as the rest of us (Porsanger, 2004) and this cultural orientation impacts cognitive processes.

COGNITIVE DIVERSITY

A resurgence of interest in cognitive linguistics in recent decades has produced extensive research indicating an undeniable link between language, culture and cognition (Evans, 2009; Hunt & Banaji, 1988; Sharifian, 2017). While previous resistance to these ideas has been necessary to defend the foundations of disciplines that initially tested only middle-class European subjects based on the supposition that cognition is universal, it is now widely accepted that cognitive processes are modified by the environment in which we grow up, the languages we speak and the cultural patterns directing our attention (Bender & Beller, 2016; Cibelli et al., 2016). Indeed, while the cognitive orientation favored globally in education is oriented towards WEIRD (Western, Educated, Industrialised, Rich, Democratic) cultures, this only represents the neurology of a minority of humans on this planet (Henrich et al., 2010).

Much of the research in this area has comprised oversimplified pseudo-science, of the 'Eskimos have 50 words for snow' variety – unhelpful but popular generalizations that divide different cultural forms of cognition into a binary of Western and non-Western paradigms (Varnum et al., 2010). However, the boundaries between these binaries are far more complex, fluid and subject to variation than these popular divisions suggest.

Multiple factors are recognised both as indicators and influencers of different cognitive orientations, including historical factors like economic change. For example, social changes brought on by globalization in places like China (Rhode et al., 2016) and Chiapas in Mexico (Greenfield et al., 2003) have resulted in a transition from interdependent to independent cultural orientations with a resultant shift from customary holistic cognition to analytical cognition.

There is considerable variation both between and within populations, particularly in Australian Aboriginal and Torres Strait Islander communities shaped by multiple generations of policies that continue to impact our lives, from extermination to protectionism to assimilation to welfare to self-determination. Additionally, for Indigenous people engaging with compulsory education, a 'double personality' is common – a shift in self-schema that is activated when code-switching between cultures, requiring a corresponding cognitive shift from interdependent to independent cognition (Rodríguez-Arauz et al., 2017).

In these complex, dynamic contexts of cultural continuity and discontinuity, consideration of multiple variables indicating different cognitive orientations (including language, environment, social patterns, cultural practice and economic activity) is desirable, particularly in designing pedagogies aligned with lived cultures that are neither static nor unified. It is important not to essentialize cultures or view them as stable entities in this work, but to recognize that they are fluid products of a history that is continuously unfolding (Iliev & Ojalehto, 2015).

Therefore, it is not possible to design or discover a universal Indigenous pedagogy framework to apply across all education institutions. The diversity of our cultural contexts, languages and experiences of colonization precludes us from producing generalizable and replicable heuristics, which may explain our difficulties in securing validation of Aboriginal pedagogy as a serious area of study in the academy. However, there are certainly clear commonalities between the diverse pedagogies of Indigenous and other non-WEIRD cultures, which account for most of the human beings on the planet.

WIK PEDAGOGIES

For the remainder of this article, I share aspects of my Wik community's cognitive orientation and identify potential areas of correlation with other Indigenous cultures, drawn from a local research project identifying ways to adapt oral culture processes for print-based learning contexts (Frazer & Yunkaporta, 2021). The findings of the project reported here are indicators of pedagogical practice found in an analysis of Wik Mungkan language, which were later validated through observation and narrative data.

Wik pedagogy is seldom a discrete practice, but involves embedding multiple disciplines, fields, and modalities in every experience of knowledge transmission. Visual and tactile learning are incorporated in the process of listening/learning in a kind of pedagogical synaesthesia. Non-verbal modalities are central, including gestures and body language, alongside place-based narratives that are walked as well as spoken. The process of becoming *ma' kuunchang*, a master in the crafting of traditional objects, involves both intense scaffolding and learner autonomy to achieve a state of inhabiting the ontology of the teacher, observing so closely in relation that the self-other boundary between instructor and learner becomes blurred. A haptic relation with place also extends to the tools used, which become part of the embodied neural processes of the learner.

While much cultural activity is divided according to gender, these general patterns are present in both male and female learning processes, revealing a learning cycle involving:

- demonstration and observation
- scaffolded and cooperative learning embedded in relationships with people and place
- explanation and deep listening enfolding narratives
- memorization employing place-based metaphors and visual schema
- demonstration of deep thinking and understanding through the production of purposeful products in real-life contexts

The term *ngaantam-ngeeyan* means to think, understand, realize, believe, decide, or evaluate. The incorporation of *ngeeyan* (listen) indicates the cultural importance of listening and orality in knowledge transmission, and the role this plays in Wik pedagogy and cognition. This aligns with Watson's (2003) insight that many Central Australian Indigenous people believe that hearing 'is the medium of intelligence' (p. 54). This is a common feature of many Indigenous Australian languages, for example, in Gamilaraay where *binna* (ear) is equated in the language with cognition and memory (Ash et al., 2003). In Wik Mungkan, there is an authority implicit in *ngeeyan* terms, an obligation for learners to show respect for knowledge holders, as in *aak ngeeyan* and *wik ngeeyan* meaning respecting and obeying.

The link between cognition and listening can also be found in idioms about memory, containing the word *kon* (ear). *Kon-ngathan* and *kon pur'* are about forgetting, while *konangam pi'-pi'an* means remembering and *kon thayanathan* means to remind. A person with a good memory is called *kon thayan* (strong ear), while a person with a learning disorder is called *weenth*, which is also the word for deaf. However, while respect and obedience may be considered an important protocol for learning and listening, this does not mean the learner has no agency.

The Wik Mungkan word for learning is *maman*, which also means to hold, touch, take from or accept what is offered. *Wik maman* (language learning) has the sense of 'picking up' a language, rather than passively learning through drills and repetition. A pedagogical orientation can be discerned here in what seems to be an attitude to learning and knowledge as something to be held, accepted discerningly by autonomous learners who play an active role in the transaction. As indicated by the terms involving *ngeeyan*, a good learner must be a good listener. The sense of agency inferred by *maman* suggests that this learner would need to be an active listener rather than passive recipient of information. *Pith mut* means the sense or meaning of words (combining the words for 'dream' and 'tail'), which is part of the phrase *pith mut ngeeyan*, meaning to understand, but more specifically to follow the meaning of what is said, which requires active engagement on the part of the listener. It also suggests an orientation to making and discerning meaning through words and language via connection with a rich practice of sensemaking connected to a spiritual reality - the 'tail of a dream.'

Basic decoding of print into sound without meaning or context would therefore result in disruptive dissonance for a learner with this cultural orientation to language learning. Pedagogical techniques are indicated by more than these kinds of inferences, however, with several terms specifically naming different kinds of knowledge transmission. For example:

- *Kon-aathan* is to train an animal using stimulu—response methods. This is the most basic pedagogy, mostly involving abrupt verbal commands and positive or negative reinforcement – similar to the default pedagogy employed by modern education and training institutions.
- *Ma'-aathan* (*ma'* meaning 'hand') is to show how to do something, teach practically using the hands, lend a 'helping hand' in a way that echoes Vygotskian scaffolding pedagogies.
- *Mee'-aathan* (*mee'* meaning 'eye') means to show, or to teach through demonstration with the learner as an active observer.
- *Thaa'-aathan* (*thaa'* meaning 'mouth') means to teach with words, especially in the teaching of language.
- *Aath*, when combined with *wuntan*, means to share, swap, exchange knowledge and things. *Aathan* is combined with different body parts to describe several *Wik* pedagogies. It means to spread, like a bushfire spreads, and is used to describe actions proceeding from one point to another, as in walk-

ing from place to place, sewing and even reading a text from top to bottom. The significance of *aathan* being used to describe print-based activities not only indicates a continuity of pedagogical practice from ancient to contemporary contexts, but also highlights the importance of specific procedural sequences in Aboriginal culture during acts of knowledge transmission.

The cultural process of proceeding from one clearly defined point, step, or location to the next is an orientation that can be seen in the singing of country through song lines (narrative maps naming the sacred places of ancestral journeys in the Dreaming). Cultural processes encoded in these songs and stories are also explicit procedural texts that give instructions in sequence (Riley, 2016). This indicates a cultural preference for explicit pedagogy and procedural learning.

LEARNING THROUGH CULTURE, NOT ABOUT IT

Although this analysis is specific to a unique Indigenous culture in a world of diverse cultures, it may be useful as a basis for inquiry allowing Indigenous teachers, scholars, and community members to express abstract ideas about customary processes they have previously been unable to articulate in Standard Australian English. This empowering process can result in an incipient meta-language for describing local pedagogies, liberating Indigenous teachers and learners from the colonizing heuristics of settler scholarship (Yunkaporta & McGinty, 2009). The ability to describe and implement Aboriginal pedagogies that may be used to teach any content as knowledge of our relations to all things in creation, rather than merely including cultural content and history in isolation, may be the key to transforming education systems for the benefit of all students and communities.

But while cultural content is easily expressed and shared in curriculum, cultural processes are often far more nebulous and difficult to describe. Culturally specific ways of thinking, knowing, and learning are often invisible to those who use them (and the outsiders who observe them), as are the cognitive frameworks of a dominant culture that must be mastered by minority cultures for economic inclusion. The key principle in utilizing Aboriginal pedagogies is that Indigenous perspectives are better provided through process rather than content alone, that students must learn *through* culture rather than *about* culture, even while studying mainstream content and acquiring essential skills needed for surviving the intrusions and rigors of the global marketplace (Yunkaporta & McGinty, 2009).

Many elements of Wik pedagogy may be generalizable to other Indigenous groups, such as the tendency for listening to be equated with understanding and cognition, which was noted earlier in the chapter to be a feature of many Aboriginal languages and cultures. It was also noted that narrative, place-based and group-oriented approaches to knowledge transmission are widely recognised as common features of Indigenous pedagogies generally. These may be points of reference to help others begin identifying similar patterns in the design of localized learning frameworks.

Indigenous languages and cultures can provide more than additional Indigenized content for inclusivity in a curriculum that is already overstuffed with mandated content. Our languages and cultures can provide rigorous processes and innovative frameworks for pedagogies and methodologies – the possibility of learning through culture from an Indigenous perspective, rather than about culture from a colonial perspective.

REFERENCES

Arnau, E., Estany, A., Gonzalez del Solar, R., & Sturm, T. (2013). The Extended Cognition Thesis: Its significance for the philosophy of (cognitive) science. *Philosophical Psychology, 27,* 1–18.

Ash, A., Giacon, J., & Lissarrague, A. (2003). *Gamilaraay, Yuwaalaraay, Yuwaalayaay dictionary.* IAD Press.

Battiste, M. (2002). *Indigenous knowledge and pedagogy in first nations education: A literature review with recommendations.* National Working Group on Education and the Minister of Indian Affairs. Ottawa: Indian and Northern Affairs Canada.

Bender, A., & Beller, S. (2016). Current perspectives on cognitive diversity. *Frontiers in Psychology, 7,* 509.

Cibelli, E., Xu, Y., Austerweil, J. L., Griffiths, T., & Regier, T. (2016). The Sapir-Whorf hypothesis and probabilistic inference: Evidence from the domain of color." *PLoS ONE, 11,* e0158725.

Curry, L. (1990). A critique of the research on learning styles. *Educational Leadership, 48*(2), 50–56.

Denny, J. P. (1983). Context in assessment of mathematical concepts from hunting societies." In J. W. Berry, S. H. Irvine, & E. B. Hunt (Eds.), *Human assessment and cultural factors* (pp. 155–161). Plenum.

Egan, K. (1998). *Teaching as story telling: An alternative approach to teaching and curriculum.* University of Chicago Press.

Evans, N. (2009). *Dying words: Endangered languages and what they have to tell us.* Wiley-Blackwell.

Frazer, B., & Yunkaporta, T. (2021). Wik pedagogies: Adapting oral culture processes for print-based contexts. *The Australian Journal of Indigenous Education, 50*(1), 88–94.

Greenfield, P., Maynard, A., & Childs, C. P. (2003). Historical change, cultural learning, and cognitive representation in Zinacantec Maya children. *Cognitive Development, 18,* 455–487.

Havelock, E. A. (1982). *The literate revolution in Greece and its cultural consequences.* Princeton University Press.

Henrich, J., Heine, S. J., & Norenzayan, A. (2010). The weirdest people in the world? *Behavioural Brain Science, 33*(2–3), 61–83; discussion 83–135.

Hughes, P., & More, A. J. (2004). *Aboriginal ways of learning.* Uni Sa Press.

Hunt, E., & Banaji, M. R. (1988). The Whorfian hypothesis revisited: A cognitive science view of linguistic and cultural effects on thought." In J. W. Berry, S. H. Irvine, & E. B. Hunt (Eds.), *Indigenous cognition: Functioning in cultural context* (pp. 57–84). Martinus Nijhoff Publishers.

Iliev, R., & Ojalehto, B. (2015). Bringing history back to culture: On the missing diachronic component in the research on culture and cognition. *Frontiers in Psychology, 6,* 716.

Marker, M. (2006). After the Makah Whale Hunt: Indigenous knowledge and limits to multicultural discourse. *Urban Education, 41*, 482–505.

Martin, D. F. (1993). *Autonomy and relatedness: An ethnography of Wik people of Aurukun, Western Cape York Peninsula.* PhD thesis. Australian National University, Canberra.

Murdoch, J. (1988). Cree cognition in natural and educational contexts. In J. W. Berry, S. H. Irvine, & E. B. Hunt (Eds.), *Indigenous cognition: Functioning in cultural context* (pp. 231–257). Martinus Nijhoff Publishers.

Porsanger, J. (2004). *An essay on indigenous methodology.* Paper Presented at the University of Tromso.

Rhode, A., Voyer, B., & Gleibs, I. (2016). Does language matter? Exploring Chinese Korean differences in holistic perception. *Frontiers in Psychology, 7*, 1508.

Riley, L. (2016). *The memory code.* Allen and Unwin.

Rodríguez-Arauz, G., Ramírez-Esparza, N., Pérez-Brena, N., & Boyd, R. L. (2017). Hablo Inglés y español: Cultural self-schemas as a function of language. *Frontiers in Psychology, 8*, 885.

Samovar, L., & Porter, R. (2004). *Communication between cultures* (5th ed.). Thompson and Wadsworth.

Sayers, B. J. (1976). *The sentence in Wik Mungkan: A description of propositional relationships.* ANU.

Sharifian, F. (2017). Cultural linguistics and linguistic relativity. *Language Sciences, 59*, 83–92.

Varnum, M., Grossmann, I., Kitayama, S., & Nisbett, R. E. (2010). The origin of cultural differences in cognition: Evidence for the social orientation hypothesis. *Current Directions in Psychological Science, 19*, 9–13.

Watson, C. (2003). *Piercing the ground.* Fremantle Arts Centre Press.

Yunkaporta, T. (2010). *Aboriginal pedagogies at the cultural interface.* Doctoral thesis. James Cook University, Qld.

Yunkaporta, T., & McGinty, S. (2009). Reclaiming Aboriginal place-based worldviews at the interface of local and non-local knowledge. *Australian Education Researcher, 36*, 55–72

Yunkaporta, T., Rae, J., & Bilton, N. (2020). A conversation about indigenous pedagogy, neuroscience and material thinking. In B. Hill, J. Harris, & R. Bacchus (Eds.), *Teaching Aboriginal cultural competence* (pp. 85–97). Springer.

CHAPTER 5

PLURALITY, EQUITY AND MEANING MAKING WITH INDIGENOUS KNOWLEDGES

Deepa Srikantaiah
University of Maryland, College Park

Brett Grant
American University

Shytance Wren
AERA (Holistic Education SIG)

This paper delves into Indigenous Knowledges, how they differ from Western scientific concepts, and their importance in education. It notes how Indigenous worldview and place-based knowledges have long been dismissed, oppressed or silenced by a hegemonic culture intending to destroy knowledge, beliefs, traditions, and language that threaten colonial assumptions. As an ultimate form of holistic education, traditional Indigenous learning methodologies, customs, and perspectives have the potential to transform systems such as school reform initiatives, curricula, budgetary goals, and incentive/disincentive structures. The essay concludes by suggesting a course of action that involves equity impact assessments that focuses on the voices, views, and principles of Indigenous Communities.

Keywords: Indigenous Knowledges, Indigenous Methodologies, Education Reform, Pedagogical Approaches

Indigenous Knowledges have long been ignored and their potential for informative decision-making continues to be undermined. In Western knowledge systems, there is a culture of epistemic violence, which seeks to maintain the status quo and resist any change in power relations by destroying systems of knowledge, beliefs, traditions, and language that challenge colonial paradigms (Dotson, 2011; Spivak, 1985). Indigenous methodologies, practices, and approaches can disrupt sociohistorical power imbalances and create equitable policymaking processes and outcomes. With the incorporation of Indigenous Knowledges, government policies, funding priorities, and incentives and disincentives associated with education reform have the opportunity to transform our society. Researchers and policymakers must actively and deliberately examine dominant cultural values and assumptions and demonstrate the importance of research beyond disciplines and knowledge established by Western scientific paradigms to include Indigenous approaches if education is ever to impact the imbalances our world is facing.

Indigenous[1] knowledge reflects knowledge that is primarily associated with Indigenous Peoples who have managed to hold on to their place-based wisdom and the in-common worldview that connects them. A common definition for Indigenous Peoples is a group of people who have a "sense of rootedness in a place" (Lee, 2003, p. 84). However, the term Indigenous and who the Indigenous are, is heavily debated in literature and practice (Dean & Levi, 2003; Niezen, 2003) because there are many communities around the world who have characteristics of Indigenous Peoples or Communities, but are not labeled as Indigenous or recognized for Indigenous rights (Dei et al., 2000; Semali & Kincheloe, 1999). There are numerous communities around the world who have long-term connections to a particular area and are not identified as "Indigenous."

Most scholars and practitioners agree that "Indigenous" Peoples have lived in a geographic area for generations and created their community based on local factors and their knowledge is culturally bound with set characteristics (Dean & Levi 2003; Dei et al., 2000; Niezen, 2003). Governments ultimately determine who is Indigenous and who deserves Indigenous rights (Srikantaiah & Rueger, 2008).[2] It is important to recognize that Indigenous Knowledges are diverse and unique from one another as they are based on the particular place from which

---

[1] Indigenous has been referred to as a historical object of colonial encounter and observations, therefore adjectives including tribal, native, aboriginal, Indian (Carnerio da Cunha & Almeila, 2000) and primitive (Niezen, 2003) are also associated with the term. Indigenous became the preferred term after 1945, the post-colonial period (Niezen, 2003).

[2] Governments in Latin America recognize various Indigenous communities. Lee (2003) says that Latin Americans have had several political and scientific discourses concerning who the Indigenous are. Maybury-Lewis (2003) adds that Mexico, Ecuador, and Bolivia have characterized themselves as "pluriethnic" countries and Mexico, for example, recognizes indigeneity and identifies 56 Indigenous communities..

they were derived. In pan-Indigenous discussions about the broader concept of worldview, it is vital to acknowledge this uniqueness of Indigenous Knowledges. Ogawa (1995) and Snively and Corsiglia (2001) note that the plurality of Indigenous Knowledges, and their association with multiple and diverse cultures, helps us understand that there are multiple approaches and perspectives to truth or reality. Indigenous Knowledges function and rely upon their environment and reflect multiple perceptions of reality (Nader, 1996; Ogawa, 1995; Snively & Corsiglia, 2001). Indigenous Knowledges are also tightly integrated with the livelihoods of local people and are not just "abstract ideas or philosophies" or "abstract representations of the world" (Agrawal, 1995, p. 422) and are "the centering of community voices and values" (Khalifa et al., 2019, p. 3).

The following characteristics can be used to identify and define place-based Indigenous Knowledges:

a. It can be considered as knowledge that is held by disadvantaged communities (Dei et al., 2000; Semali & Kincheloe, 1999);
b. It is knowledge that may be undocumented or orally passed from generation to generation by elders in a community (Dei et al., 2000; Ogawa, 1995; Semali & Kincheloe, 1999);
c. It is generally not knowledge learned in formal education systems or is not circulated in university settings (Sillitoe, 2002);
d. It generally reflects its originality despite historical wars, imperialism, colonization, and modernization events (Dei et al., 2000; Semali & Kincheloe, 1999);
e. It includes cultural perspectives, beliefs, mythological stories, and lived experiences in social and natural environments (Kawakami, 1998; Snively & Corsiglia, 2001);[3]
f. It is a reflection of interconnectedness of mind, body, spirit, community, and place that remains under attack by hegemonic forces.

INDIGENOUS KNOWLEDGES AND WESTERN SCIENTIFIC PARADIGMS

Western science, or the dominant thinking in science, does not generally acknowledge the interdependence that Indigenous Knowledges have with their environment, nor how the wisdom practice is nurtured via language, rituals, and ceremonies. For example, during periods of colonization, French, English, and Spanish colonists introduced 'reductionist' medicine as the solution to health problems

---

[3] Certain Indigenous Knowledges, although also having been oppressed by colonization or modernization, are dominant and may undermine minoritized members of a society. The caste system in India is an example.

in their colonies (Shroff, 2000).[4] Reductionist medicine undermined social aspects of Indigenous knowledge including Indigenous religions, oral traditions, and traditional healers which were originally used for healthcare. The reductionist concept, influenced by Cartesian philosophy, implies that the human body is simply a mechanical system, and each compartment operates and functions separately (Ogawa, 1995). Reductionist medicine also includes the implementation of Western hospitals, promoting the dissemination of allopathic medicines and some homeopathic medicines, and the design of healthcare systems based solely on Western science.

Such perceived supremacy of Indigenous Knowledges causes them to be marginalized in research and funding because their philosophies do not align with Western scientific methods (Briggs & Sharp, 2004; Jegede, 1999; Ogawa, 1995; Snively & Corsiglia, 2001). Rationales often relate to references that laud the west's "miracle drugs," like the polio vaccination, which has helped eliminate polio in many parts of the world and was relied on as the benchmark to validate other forms of knowledge and their approaches to treatment (Briggs & Sharp, 2004).[5] Of course, the medicinal knowledge of Indigenous Peoples remains largely ignored while simultaneously being commercially taken without the accompanying spiritual knowledge used as curatives for most of human history.

With the philosophical understanding that there are multiple perspectives to truth, it is important to acknowledge that Indigenous Knowledges can complement Western science. For example, essiac, a plant found on tree bark and used by Ojibwe people to treat diseases such as cancer, "contains inulin, an enzyme that breaks down the mucous coating on cancer cells and allows the body's defensive system to enter them" (Rosenberg, 2000, p. 147). Understanding the plurality of knowledge in our world can enhance the global scientific dialogue, not by Western competition, but by the non-dualistic Indigenous Worldview that seeks complementarity in all apparent opposites. Uncovering the synergies across knowledges is fundamental to help bridge gaps (Jegede, 1999). Working peacefully together, we can be allies who use the totality of our knowledges to benefit society.

Although some believe that such partnerships between Western education and Indigenous education cannot happen, others believe that Western education and Indigenous approaches to curriculum and instruction can "go hand-in-hand." Moreover, some believe education is the only way for "transmitting, amassing, enhancing, and altering" Indigenous Knowledges (Easton, 2004, p. 1). Unfortunately, Western education systems impose a "specialized set of educational ex-

---

[4] Civilizations have, "thrived for millennia completely outside the realm of Western science, agriculture, and belief systems, [and] offer truly alternative views of ecology and agriculture that stem from long-term use and conservation of natural resources" (Norton et al., 1998, p. 333).

[5] Vaccines are also a reductionist approach to treatment and a humanitarian response to emergency healthcare situations. Vaccines are not holistic or a long-term health approach, which reflect philosophies of Indigenous Knowledges, and in addition long-term effects of vaccines on immunity and wellbeing is not well researched.

periences that are discontinuous with those encountered in daily life and [that] supports ways of learning and thinking that are frequently antithetical to those fostered by practical daily experiences" (Scribner & Cole, 1973, p. 553).

While education systems are constantly improving, the knowledge produced is biased toward Western ideas, views, and values. The field of education consists of a combination of different social and cultural principles that change overtime. However, these principles that prevail are based on neoliberal ideals, which are manifestations of Western thinking. With the spread of compulsory education, the expansion of education scale, and the strengthening of the role of the state in education, education has increasingly entailed the philosophies of Western knowledge. The emphasis is on efficiency and monetized values over diversity, equity, well-being, and care.

British colonization has also influenced global education standards, including the United States, and colonialism in education is still prominent today (Abdi, 2011). Neocolonialism and neoliberalism continue to shape educational structures and processes. Anglophone regimes and much of western Europe have accepted neocolonialism to run global economies. The political, social, and economic philosophies of neocolonialism and neoliberalism, along with other Western theories such as human capital, state theory, world culture theory, and modernity, promote unequal knowledge distribution (Takayama et al., 2017). A primary means by which Western knowledge was asserted as universal was the denigration and denial of non-Western ways of knowing (Santos, 2007). As described in Santos' (2002) theory of the Sociology of Absences, there is a deliberate and systematic erasure of Indigenous Knowledges to deem it as an inconceivable alternative to what is presumed to exist. The Washington Consensus, for example, impacted the democratic governance of developing countries, intensified inequality, and hurt the marginalized (Whyte, 2019) by initiating and enforcing development through Western paradigms. For example, within the Washington Consensus, many Western organizations' international rankings and evaluation systems use Western education criteria.

Indigenous Knowledges have important pedagogical approaches, or learning models or patterns, that are related to other local environments and cultures of communities. Unfortunately, many school curricula are designed largely outside the context of Indigenous groups, with little regard to their cultures. Education policies and practices can promote Indigenous Knowledges, cultures, values, and identity through the instruction of Indigenous languages. However, utilizing Indigenous Knowledge, should go beyond just vocabulary or grammatical rules and involve the transfer of philosophies, histories, and customs as well. Ahenakew (2016) warns against "grafting", whereby other knowledge traditions are incorporated into curricula only after being transplanted onto Western knowledge systems or manipulated to meet mainstream institutional goals (p. 323). Grafting for inclusion does not happen as a mutually beneficial exercise, but rather as a form of assimilation (Ahenakew, 2016). Using this approach, Indigenous perspectives and peoples are recognized and included only if they are compatible with Western paradigms and do not threaten the epistemological hegemony of Western institutions. Rather than transplanting and manipulating Indigenous Knowledges, the emphasis should instead be on an 'ecology of knowledges' that recognizes the 'plurality of heterogeneous knowledges (one of them being modern science) and on the sustained and dynamic interconnections between them without compromising their autonomy' (Santos, 2007, p. 11).

REFERENCES

Abdi, A. A. (Ed.). (2011). *Decolonizing philosophies of education.* Sense Publishers.

Agrawal, A. (1995). Dismantling the divide between indigenous and scientific knowledge." *Development and Change, 26*(3), 413–439.

Ahenakew, C. (2016). Grafting Indigenous ways of knowing onto non-Indigenous ways of being: The (underestimated) challenges of a decolonial imagination. *International Review of Qualitative Research,* 9(3), 323–340.

Briggs, J., & Sharp, J. (2004). Indigenous knowledges and development: A postcolonial caution. *Third World Quarterly, 25*(4), 661–676.

Carnerio de Cunha, M., & Mauro W., de Almeida, B. (2000). Indigenous people, traditional people, and conservation in the Amazon. *Brazil: The Burden of the past; The Promise of the Future, 129*(2), 315–338.

Dean, B., & Levi, J. M. (Eds.). (2003). *At the risk of being heard: Identity, indigenous rights, and postcolonial states.* The University of Michigan Press.

Dei, G., Hall, B., & Rosenberg, D. G. (Eds.). (2000). *Indigenous knowledge in global contexts: Multiple readings of our world.* University of Toronto Press.

Dotson, K. (2011). Tracking epistemic violence, tracking practices of silencing. *Hypatia, 26*(2), 236–257.

Easton, P. (2004). Education and indigenous knowledge. IK Note. In *Local pathways to global development.* World Bank.

Jegede, O. (1999). Science education in non-western cultures: Towards a theory of collateral learning. In L. Semali & J. Kincheloe (Eds.), *What is indigenous knowledge? Voices from the academy* (pp. 119–142). Falmer Press.

Kawakami, A. J. (1998). Sense of place, community, and identity: Bridging the gap between home and school for Hawaiian students. *Education and Urban Society, 32*(1).

Khalifa, M. A., Khalil, D., Marsh, T. E., & Holloran, C. (2019). Toward an indigenous, decolonizing school leadership: A literature review." *Educational Administration Quarterly, 55*(4), 1–44.

Lee, R. B. (2003). Indigenous rights and the politics of identity in post-apartheid Southern Africa. In B. Dean & J. M. Levi (Eds.), *At the risk of being heard identity, indigenous rights, and postcolonial states* (pp. 80–111). The University of Michigan Press.

Maybury-Lewis, D. (2003). From elimination to an uncertain future: Changing policies toward indigenous peoples. In B. Dean & J. M. Levi (Eds.), *At the risk of being heard identity, indigenous rights, and postcolonial states* (pp. 324–334). The University of Michigan Press.

Nader, L. (1996). Anthropological inquiry into boundaries, power, knowledge. In L. Nader (Ed.), *Naked science* (pp. 1–25). Routledge.

Niezen, R. (2003). *The origins of Indigenism.* University of California Press.

Norton, J. B., Pawluk, R. R., & Sandor, J. A. (1998). Observation and experience linking science and indigenous knowledge at Zuni, New Mexico. *Journal of Arid Environments, 39*(2), 331–340.

Ogawa, M. (1995). Science education in a multiscience perspective. *Science Education, 79*(5), 583–593.

Rosenberg, D. G. (2000). Toward indigenous wholeness: Feminist praxis in transformative learning on health and the environment. In G. Dei, B. Hall, & D. G. Rosenberg, *indigenous knowledge in global contexts: Multiple readings of our world* (pp. 137–154). University of Toronto Press.

Santos, B. de S. (2002). Para uma sociologia das ausências e uma sociologia das emergências [On the emergency of a sociology of absences]. *Revista Crítica de Ciências Sociais, 63*, 237–280.

Santos, B. de S. (2007). Beyond abyssal thinking: From global lines to ecologies of knowledges." *Review (Fernand Braudel Center), 20*(1), 45–89.

Scribner, S., & Cole, M. (1973). Cognitive consequences of formal and informal education. *Science, 182*(4112), 553–559.

Semali, L., & Kincheloe, J. (Eds.). (1999). *What is indigenous knowledge? Voices from the Academy*. Falmer Press.

Shroff, F. M. (2000). Ayurveda: Mother of indigenous health knowledge. In G. Dei, B. Hall, & D. G. Rosenberg (Eds.), *Indigenous knowledge in global contexts: Multiple readings of our world* (pp. 215–233). University of Toronto Press.

Sillitoe, P. (2002). Globalizing indigenous knowledge. In P. Sillitoe, A. Bricker, & Johan Pottier (Eds.), *Participating in development approaches to indigenous knowledge* (pp. 108–138). Routledge Taylor and Francis Group.

Snively, G., & Corsiglia, J. (2001). Discovering indigenous science: Implications for science education. *Science Education, 85*(1), 6–34.

Spivak, G. C. (1985). The Rani of Sirmur: An essay in reading the archives. *History and Theory, 24*(3), 247–272.

Srikantaiah, D., & Rueger, C. (2008). An alternative knowledge system at the World Bank: A case study of the indigenous knowledge for development program. In T. K. Srikantaiah, & Koeing, M. *Knowledge management in practice: Context and connection*. Information Today, Inc.

Takayama, K., Sriprakash, A., & Connell, R. (2017). Toward a postcolonial comparative and international education. *Comparative Education Review, 61*(S1), S1–S24.

Whyte, J. (2019). *The morals of the market: Human rights and the rise of neoliberalism*. Verso Books.

CHAPTER 6

LAKOTA EPISTEMOLOGY AS HOLISTIC BEING

Ethleen Iron Cloud Two Dogs
Oglala Mental Health Project; Oglala Women's Equity Movement

In this article, the author describes Lakota epistemology in ways that reveal its natural "holistic" dimensions. Referring to Indigenous ways of knowing, healing and spirituality, she offers examples of how they are each the embodiment of holistic understandings.

Keywords: Lakota Epistemology, Relationality, Lakota Language

Several thousand years ago, the only cherished son of a Lakota man and Lakota woman went out to hunt one day and did not return. The family looked for him and could not find him. They called upon a *Wakan Iyeska* (Wah-kunh Ee-yeh-skah, Interpreter of the Sacred) who called upon his spirit helpers to help locate the boy. The family was told in ceremony where to look for him and they could not find him. They went back to the *Wakan Iyeska* who told them he is there where you were told to look. When they searched again, they saw a bush with red branches and they were told, that is him, that is your son – he gave his life so that the people would have a medicine, *c'an s'a s'a* (chunh shah shah, red willow bark) for sacred tobacco offerings. The red color in the bark is the blood of the relative that gave his life.

This story reveals how reciprocity is critical to the Lakota. To this day, the Lakota people gather the red willow branches during the appropriate time of year and prepare it for use in their *c'anunpa* (sacred pipe). The plant, *c'an s'a s'a* (red willow bark used for a natural tobacco offering) could be seen as an inanimate object but the origin of where the plant came from is a reminder to the people to treat all life as sacred and as relatives, a tenet central to Lakota epistemology. It shows that relationships form the foundation for how to function and thrive in the world; respecting and honoring all forms of sacred life was taught as a way to keep in balance.

A prime example of the sacredness of life was how Lakota children are traditionally viewed as gifts from the Creator and as the life blood of the future of the people. Thus, every opportunity to enhance their growth – physically, mentally, emotionally, spiritually – was taken as a responsibility to support them in reaching their full potential and fulfill their purpose in life. Lakota people refer to the unborn child as "*hoksi nagi*" (spirit child) and not as a fetus, baby, or child. The general Lakota term for boy and girl child is "Wakanyeja," or "as a sacred being.

This is because it is believed that the child exists as a spiritual being prior to being born to the earth. The mother was protected by the extended family thereby protecting the *hoksi nagi*. Once the *hoksi nagi* came to the physical realm of the earth, then he or she traveled through seven stages of life from spirit in womb, to infant, to child, to youth, to adult, to elder and then to spirit again.

Each stage of life has teachings, protocols, and ceremonies that correspond to the age range within each stage. For example, the *Hoksicila* stage began with a grandmother welcoming the infant to the world, bestowing a blessing on the infant, giving thanks to the Creator for the gift, and making a prediction for the life of the infant as he or she makes the journey through each stage. The *Wakanyeja* ("as a sacred being") was treated as sacred, never being hit and always being spoken to gently, which was a reflection of the belief of their sacredness. Conduct toward the child was governed by the belief that the child's spirit could turn around and return to the spirit world at any time. The epistemology, or ways of knowing, of the Lakota people included great reverence for higher spiritual powers. The belief that those higher spiritual powers could influence the journey of the child on earth or contribute to an untimely return to the spirit world was given great credence.

While Cajete (2005) asserted there is no American Indian translation for epistemology, epistemology would be explained in the Lakota language as *"Lakol Wiyeya Pi"* (a collective knowledge and worldview). The story about how the Lakota people received the gift of the *c'an c'an s'a s'a* (red willow) is one example. It has been passed down from generation to generation and provides a framework for *"o'han"* (a way of being or how to conduct oneself). Lessons can be taken from this seemingly simple story such as honoring kinship. Those that know and honor the teachings from the story relate to the *c'an s'a s'a* as a relative by offering tobacco and a prayer before harvesting the plant.

Nakata et al. (2005) make a critical point that traditional knowledge of Indigenous peoples includes both past and continuing knowledge. Sadly, we are losing our traditional knowledge. Each generation is being moved away from nature's spiritual energy and pathways. Through honoring this Lakota teaching, individuals learn the importance of *"wayuonihan,"* the concept of honoring self and others so that life can continue.

Deloria and Wildcat (2001) observed that the parameters of American Indian knowledge were based on not what is believed to be true or correct but on respect. Kovach (2010, p. 41) refers to it as "knowledge nested within the social relations of knowledge production." The aspects of interconnectedness and relationality in North American Indian philosophy are foundational cornerstones (Bishop, 1999; Deloria, 1999) discussing the underpinnings of Indigenous knowledge, Cajete stated that,

> Indians throughout the Americas incorporate a number of symbolic expressions that reflect the metaphysical, ecological, and cultural constructs of tribal epistemology. These symbolic constructs, when translated, include the following: Tree of Life, Earth Mother, Sun Father, Sacred Twins, Mother of Game or Corn, Old Man, Trickster, Holy Wind or Life's Sake, We Are All Related, Completed Man/Woman, the Great Mystery, Life Way, and Sacred Directions. These expressions, which occur in a variety of forms in nearly all-American Indian languages, reflect common understandings and shared foundations for traditional ways of learning. That is, behind each of these mythic metaphors are the philosophical infrastructures and fields of tribal knowledge that lie at the heart of American Indian epistemologies. (Cajete, 2005, pp. 72–73)

The ultimate representation of the Lakota metaphysical, ecological and cultural understanding is our phrase, *"Mitakuye Oyasin,"* which means "We Are All Related." It reflects the deep holism and holistic nature of Lakota knowledge for all aspects of life: physical, mental, emotional, spiritual, space and place. For example, Lakota people believe they are part of the universe with a responsibility to be a "good relative" to all, not only humans but all entities including the nations of four-legged, winged, stones, plants, trees, stars, spirit beings, ghosts, water, and fire. Traditional Lakota knowledge is exemplified in the day-to-day behavior and conduct, in the ceremonial lifeways and through songs and stories.

STORYTELLING AND COMMUNICATION IN LAKOTA EPISTEMOLOGY

Brant Castellano (2004, p. 100) explained "Traditional teachings are conveyed through example, through stories and songs, in ceremonies and, most importantly, through engagement with the natural world which is governed by laws of life just as human beings are." Vernon (2012), related how stories help "Native people learn who they are, where they come from, and how to act." An example is the story of how a group of Lakota people living in a *Wicoti* (camp) were starving so a young man set out to find food for his people. He was sent with a little food to sustain him on his journey, he came upon a *Ti Ikciye* (common dwelling or Tipi) where an old woman lived by herself. She related that she had nothing to eat so he offered the food he had to her. She told him that because he was generous, he would always have food. As he went on his way, he looked in his pack and seen that he had an abundance of food which sustained him throughout his journey. He then came upon another *Ti Ikciye* and there was a beautiful young woman living there, she invited him to take shelter in her *Ti Ikciye*. They fell in love, but the man knew he had to continue his journey to find food for his people. He told her he had to leave, she said she would go with him and help him, and they became companions for life. During part of their journey, the spirit of the Sun spoke to the man telling him that if he danced before him (the sun) and shed his blood on the ground then his prayers would be answered.

The characters of the old woman and the sun in the story show the importance of having regard for Elders and of seeking and following spiritual guidance as part of life's journey. The teachings in the story emphasize the values of "*Ihakicikta*" (looking out for others), "Wacante Ognaka" (generosity), "*tohan ni ya pi*" (being together for life, a value taken from the Eagle relatives), "okiciya pi" (helping one another) and "*Icicu pi*" (sacrificing self for others, as in the Sundance ceremony). A contemporary representation of the value of *Ihakicikta* is shown by Dennis (2014, p. 44) in her study on grief and loss among Lakota Elders; she identified "collective responsibility" as a critical dynamic that the Elders shared in response to tragic community events.

Stories handed down through the generations were transmitted orally and seen by mainstream society as folklore, mythology, and without actual substance. Brayboy (2005) discussed how the value of stories and narratives were minimized, "locating theory as something absent from stories and practices is problematic in many Indigenous communities and in the work of anthropologists who seek to represent Indigenous communities" (p. 426). The theory was that storytelling "honors orality as a means of transmitting knowledge and upholds the relational..." (Brayboy, 2005, p. 42) and was an effective way to convey a message that would promote Lakota ways of being that were grounded in the value of being a good relative to all Wilson, 2008).

FACTORS OF LANGUAGE AND COMMUNICATION IN LAKOTA EPISTEMOLOGY

Lakota holistic knowledge is rooted in Indigenous language. It has much deeper meaning than what can be conveyed in English. For example, "*wa cante ognaka*" is translated as "generosity" but the term actually means "to hold others in the heart." It signifies the importance of being generous and sharing with others, which guards against materialism and individualism and promotes a relational world view where everyone and everything is given consideration. The Lakota language is concept based, that is, a few words can speak volumes. For example, a drawn out *"ohaanh"* signifies "I hear you, I empathize"; a male expressing sadness and regret while listening to your tale of misfortune might say, *"hown."* Knowing that you are being heard and listened to, that someone is fully present for you can be healing.

Lakota ways of knowing included expressions of communication as in euphemisms and metaphors in the Lakota language that are intended to influence the conduct in a diplomatic, indirect way. Cajete (2005, p. 72) stated that "… most traditional knowledge was contextualized in the day-to-day life experience of the people. For example, *"tuweni hecu sni"* ("no one does that"), was a common term used to let a person know that what they did or are doing is against protocol. The consequences of acting in a manner unbecoming of Lakota value driven conduct was often attributed to *Wakunza*, or "supernatural retribution" (Grobsmith, 1974). For example, when a person stole something, the retribution believed to be influenced by the spiritual powers, was that the person would lose two or three times as much the value of what was stolen.

Lakota ways of knowing in communication guided the people in when, where and how to express themselves to assure being in balance. Young people would not express themselves publicly without seeking permission from Elders or without excusing themselves before Elders. It was thought that the Elders had more of a right to speak publicly based on their wisdom generated by years of lived experience. Part of that wisdom was to be deliberate with words and thoughts. The term *"i-ni wakan,"* a Lakota term that means, loosely translated, what comes out of your mouth is sacred. This meant the person's words had to be carefully chosen as the words have a spirit and can have great impact, positive or negative, on whomever they are directed at. Gossip was strongly discouraged as individuals were told that the spirit of those words would make a circle and come back to them.

COMMUNICATING WITH THE SPIRITS

Spirit is inseparable from Lakota life ways and communication with the spirit world is a natural and continual practice for those who still remember the old way. It is a way to stay in tune with the environment and all of creation in the universe. When Lakota people hunted a buffalo, for example, they would prepare for the hunt spiritually because they knew the buffalo are spiritual relatives. They would make prayers and offerings to the Pte Oyate (buffalo nation) asking them to give up one of their relatives so that the people would live. Once they hunted the buffalo, they would make a tobacco offering to the spirit of the buffalo, and then drink the blood as they considered every part of the buffalo as medicine. They would then observe the pancreas of the buffalo, in which the thickness of the organ would indicate whether the winter would be harsh or mild. This knowledge was passed down through the generations as a way of knowing how to prepare for the coming winter.

The seasons and the spiritual calendar guided the Lakota people as a way of knowing what to do and when to do it. The late Matthew Bear Shield, Oglala Lakota Wakan Iyeska (Interpreter of the Sacred) strongly asserted that "When we followed the Lakota ways and spiritual laws of the universe, the people flourished. Because we went away from the Lakota spiritual calendar, our people suffer and are in chaos" (Robertson et al., 2004, p. 499). Observing and following the spiritual calendar kept the people in balance and in tune with the universe. For example, when the sun passed through the constellation of the *Wincincala Sakowin* (seven little girls) during the Spring Equinox, the Lakota people knew it was time to fill their sacred pipes and pray to welcome back the Thunder Beings and ask for their compassion as well. This particular constellation and ceremony is associated with a sacred site in the Black Hills called *Hinhan Kaga Paha* (Imitates Owl Mountain).

Keeping in balance with human relatives and all other entities, life forms and spirit forms in the universe was the foundation for the laws, values, customs and beliefs of the Lakota people. There was an inherent belief in providing children with a well-rounded Lakota cultural education so they would have the knowledge, fortitude and wisdom to navigate the *Oinajin Topa* (Four Stages of Life) on earth and live to become a *Winuhcala* (Elder woman) or *Wicahcala* (Elder man) so they can pass on the cultural and spiritual teachings of the Lakota people.

I want to note that writing about Indigenous stories and spiritual teachings is risky. Davis (2004) posits that stories help us understand the world, ourselves and as ways to communicate, but cautions of the risks in writing about Indigenous stories including compromising the integrity of stories by creating opportunities for readers to misinterpret, decontextualize, or offend Indigenous knowledge holders who believe certain stories should not be written about. Lakota epistemology is no different. There are ways of knowing that belong to certain societies among the Lakota, and that only Lakota's who know the language and ceremony can talk about or discuss. There is Lakota knowledge that cannot be written down nor discussed publicly, particularly in the realm of spirituality.

Lakol Wiyeya Pi (a collective knowledge and worldview) encompasses a broad and complex network of elements that include ways of knowing related to philosophy, communication, religion, astronomy or star knowledge, relationships, science, arts and spirituality. It also has a fluid nature that precludes categorizing these elements. The evolving nature of Lakota epistemology is evident in the way that Elders seen a need to develop a Lakota cultural model that addressed individuals, particularly children, who were out of balance and disconnected from their Lakota cultural lifeways. This imbalance and disconnection is reflected in the following examples where children, once regarded and treated as "sacred beings" are now suffering unspeakable violations and exposure to violence and trauma.

I close by saying that the Indigenous worldview, as represented by the unique place-based Lakota knowledge, is the foundation for what is being called "holistic education." As such, holistic education cannot work in a colonized context that over-emphasizes the dominant worldview over the Indigenous one. The tragic consequences of the loss of the Lakota way of knowing and the disregard for our Indigenous worldview foretell of what is in store for all life on Mother Earth.

REFERENCES

Bishop, R. (1999). Kaupapa Maori research: An indigenous approach to creating knowledge. In Robertson, N. (Ed). *Maori and psychology: Research and practice* (pp.1–6). Proceedings of a symposium sponsored by the Maori & Psychology Research Unit, Department of Psychology, University of Waikato, Hamilton, Thursday 26th August 1999 Hamilton, New Zealand: Māori and Psychology Research Unit, University of Waikato. https://waik-rg-prod.its.waikato.ac.nz/bitstream/handle/10289/874/1999%20Bishop.pdf?sequence=1&isAllowed=y

Brant Castellano, M. (2004). Ethics of Aboriginal research. *Journal of Aboriginal Health*, *1*(1), 98–114.

Brayboy, B. (2005). Toward a tribal critical race theory in education. *Urban Review*, *37*(5), 425–446. doi:10.1007/s11256-005-0018-y

Cajete, G. (2005). American Indian epistemologies. *New Directions for Student Services*, *109*, 69–78.

Davis, L. (2004). Risky stories: Speaking and writing in colonial spaces. *Native Studies Review*, *15*(1), 1–20.

Deloria, V. (1999). *Spirit & reason: The Vine Deloria, Jr. reader*. Fulcrum Publishing.

Deloria, V., & Wildcat, D. R. (2001). *Power and place: Indian education in America*. Fulcrum Publishing.

Dennis, M. K. (2014). Layers of loss, death, and grief as social determinants of Lakota elders' behavioral health. *Best Practices in Mental Health*, *10*(2), 32. https://link.gale.com/apps/doc/A439363087/HRCA?u=anon~5e22d1d8&sid=googleScholar&xid=b45715c2

Grobsmith, E. S. (1974). Wakunza: Uses of Yuwipi medicine power in contemporary Teton Dakota culture. *Plains Anthropologist*, *19*(64), 129–133.

Kovach, M. (2010). Conversation method in indigenous research. *First Peoples Child & Family Review*, *5*(1), 40–48. https://fpcfr.com/index.php/FPCFR/article/view/172

Nakata, M., Byrne, A., Nakata, V., & Gabrielle, G. (2005). Indigenous knowledge, the library and information service sector, and protocols. *Australian Academic & Research Libraries*, *36*(2), 9–24.

Robertson, P., Jorgensen, M., & Garrow, C. (2004). Indigenizing evaluation research: How Lakota methodologies are helping 'raise the tipi' in the Oglala Sioux nation. *The American Indian Quarterly*, *28*(3&4), 499–526.

Vernon, I. S. (2012). 'We were those who walked out of bullets and hunger': Representation of trauma and healing in 'solar storms.' *American Indian Quarterly*, *36*(1), 34–49.

Wilson, S. (2008). *Research is ceremony: Indigenous research methods*. Fernwood Publishing.

CHAPTER 7

HOW IT MIGHT HAVE BEEN

Devona Lone Wolf

Oglala Lakota College, Kyle, SD

In this short opinion piece, Devona Lone Wolf suggests that the holistic approach to learning that typified Indigenous cultures was a threat to the colonizing interests of the United States federal government. She suggests that our world might not be facing so many global crises if instead of designing boarding schools to force assimilation into the Western worldview, the holistic Indigenous approaches to education would have been invited into American school systems.

Keywords: Holistic Approaches, Western Education, Indigenous Education, Indigenous Worldview

After the end of treaty making between the United States and Native Americans in 1871, the U.S. government began an aggressive movement to "civilize" the natives. This time was called the "boarding school era." Lt. Col. Richard Henry Pratt led the effort for off-reservation boarding schools with the goal of forced assimilation. Native children were separated from their families and placed in government- or church-sponsored schools that were funded by the government. The Indian boarding schools were one of the primary weapons used to break down Indian identity during this period by forbidding Native languages and culture at every turn. Native American children were forcibly removed from their families and communities and sent to these schools. They were required to learn English, adopt European-American cultural practices, and convert to Christianity.

Most people know about the tragedy of the boarding schools in the U.S. and Canada, so I will not say more about the horrors that we have learned about them. Rather, I want to assert that Pratt's well-intended goals were really ultimately an attack on the holistic education that made the Indian an Indian. I describe his goals as well-intended because his speech at the National Conference of Charities and Correction in June of 1892 reveals that he believed previous treatment of the Indians was inhumane. I offer a few quotes from the speech that show this, as well as his foundational belief in the inferiority of traditional Indigenous ways of understanding the interconnectedness of all. The title of his speech was "The Advantages of Mingling Indians with Whites" (Carlisle Indian School Resource Center, 1892).

Pratt opens his presentation saying: "A great general has said that the only good Indian is a dead one, and that high sanction of his destruction has been an enormous factor in promoting Indian massacres. In a sense, I agree with the sentiment, but only in this: that all the Indian there is in the race should be dead. Kill the Indian in him, and save the man...." He goes on to describe George Washington's original policy of "association, equality and amalgamation-killing the Indian and saving the man." He refers to the sadness and inhumanity of government troops killing Indians, but says it is "a far sadder day for them when they fall under the baneful influences of a treaty agreement with the United States whereby, they are to receive large annuities, and to be protected on reservations, held apart from all association with the best of our civilization." He then criticizes Indian schools because they are:

> ...well calculated to keep the Indians intact as Indians...we shall not succeed in Americanizing the Indian... It is a great mistake to think that the Indian is born an inevitable savage. He is born a blank, like all the rest of us. Left in the surroundings of savagery, he grows to possess a savage language, superstition, and life. We, left in the surroundings of civilization, grow to possess a civilized language, life, and purpose. Transfer the infant white to the savage surroundings, he will grow to possess a savage language, superstition, and habit. Transfer the savage-born infant to the surroundings of civilization, and he will grow to possess a civilized language and habit. These results have been established over and over again beyond all question; and it is also well established that those advanced in life, even to maturity, of either class, lose the already acquired qualities belonging to the side of their birth, and gradually take on those of the side to which they have been transferred.

Besides Pratt's ignorance of the interconnected, holistic, and nature-based perspective of the Native American was demonstrated by most of the Indian agents of the U.S. government. For example, consider the words of John S. Ward, an Indian agent for the Mission Agency in California:

> The parents of these Indian children are ignorant, and know nothing of the value of education, and there are no elevating circumstances in the home circle to arouse the

ambition of the children. Parental authority is hardly known or exercised among the Indians in this agency. The agent should be endowed with some kind of authority to enforce attendance. The agent here has found that a threat to depose a captain if he does not make the children attend school has had a good effect. (Bear, 2008)

How different might our world be today if Pratt and the missionaries and the Indian agents understood the Indigenous worldview approach to education? What if the hierarchical, materialistic, anthropocentric orientation of the European colonizers was seen as the foundation for education that needed to take on the attributes of the Indian? A foundation based on the following characteristics of teaching and learning:

- Education is a holistic process that encompasses academic knowledge and physical, emotional, spiritual, and cultural development.
- Education is about transmitting cultural values, traditions, and practices relating to the interconnectedness of all, from one generation to the next.
- Indigenous education is grounded in respect, responsibility, and reciprocity.
- Indigenous education is structured with a strong emphasis on community involvement and the role of the community in shaping and guiding the education of its members.
- Indigenous education also strongly emphasizes experiential learning, with a focus on hands-on, place-based learning rooted in the local environment and culture.

My own teaching philosophy at Oglala Lakota College is based on the Lakota concept that we are all equal, but each is on their own path for gaining knowledge and skills. I imagine land stretching in all directions with some valleys and mountains. There are many paths going in all directions. Some zigzag back and forth, others go in a straight line, and some even turn sideways and backward. On these paths, there is darkness and light, storms and sunlight. These represent each individual's path traveled throughout the life journey. On these paths, everyone gains knowledge that can be shared ultimately for the greater good. From this perspective we all have the opportunity to learn from another because the knowledge gained in life experiences gives way to wisdom.

No one person can experience all the paths, and this is why everyone in a group or community contributes to the learning process that includes an equal emphasis on mind, body, emotions, spirit, community, place and "all our relations." Such holistic education is proven sustainable in all ways and there were some unbiased European observers of Native Americans who recognized this, without romanticizing them. If instead of trying to "kill" this perspective to "Americanize" the "savage," the U.S. government would have set up schools that taught Indigenous holistic ways of being and merged them with some of the "good paths of experience" that came from Europe, perhaps we would not be facing the many crises that all people, not just Native Americans, are started to suffer.

In recent years, there has been a growing movement to acknowledge and address the harm caused by Indian boarding schools and to honor the resilience and strength of Native American communities. However, few understand how we have managed to walk in both educational worlds. I close this piece by offering four perspectives that will help the reader better understand how the Lakota and other First Nations perceived boarding school education. Historically.

The first perspective was, of course, negative and led to resistance efforts. Families hid the children five years or older to protect them from the government officials who came into the villages and forcefully took the children. Following this, the next perspective was about survival. It was born from the hardships the Natives suffered from the forced removal from their lands and from being put into what essentially were prisoner of war camps (reservations). In 1899, the U.S. government named my reservation, Pine Ridge, POW Camp 334. Families continue to this day struggling to provide for their children, but then food was completely inadequate and often spoiled. During this time many families saw boarding schools as a way for their children to receive food, shelter, and clothing. They understood their children would lose their language and culture and would not receive the nurturing they would get at home. It was a tough decision that many of them had to make.

The third perspective was based on the eventual realization and acceptance that to survive in the white man's world, children needed to learn how to live in that world. Boarding schools were viewed as a way for their children to learn the white man's ways and come home and help the oyate (people) to adjust to the ways of the white world. Sadly, many children who attended boarding schools and lost their "Indianness" came home to find out they no longer fit or were accepted back into the tribe. As more and more of them attended boarding schools and returned, it became easier to adjust and be accepted. Over time the boarding school boarded students and had day students who lived at home but attended schools.

The fourth and current perspective might be that we are sort of continuing the "day" school attitude but beginning to challenge the hegemony with efforts to restore cultural relevance and save our original languages. Other non-Indian individuals attempt to help with this with critical pedagogy, holistic education and decolonizing education. While education has improved in many ways, it nonetheless remains hegemonic and violates the deep holistic approach to learning that truly allows people to recognize everything is related and important.

REFERENCES

Carlisle Indian School Resource Center. (1892). https://doi.org/10.4159/harvard.9780674435056.c39

Charla Bear. (2008). *American Indian boarding schools haunt many.* NPR. https://www.npr.org/2008/05/12/16516865/american-indian-boarding-schools-haunt-many#:~:text=Col.-,Richard%20H.,the%20race%20should%20be%20dead.%22

CHAPTER 8

EMBRACING SACREDNESS IN EDUCATION

Indigenous Psychology and the Seven Daily Walks

Arthur W. Blume

Washington State University, Pullman, WA,

Indigenous American Psychology believes that the universe ("Creation") is sacred and that its entities share in that sacredness. Learning from the sacred universe, a lifelong process necessary to becoming a healthy human being, is viewed as a sacred activity. Viewing Creation as sacred, along with the assumptions of interdependence and egalitarianism of Creation's sacred entities, suggests important implications for educational processes and content. The paper that follows introduces how these concepts and values may help to transform and decolonize education, altering how, what, and why we educate. Although it may take generations to transform societies into equitable and just social systems, it is posited that Indigenizing learning may provide an effective method to educate toward a more just society.

Keywords: Colonial Education, Daily Educational Walks, Spiritual Centeredness, Decolonization, Decolonizing Education

INTRODUCTION

Education has been idealistically viewed as a virtuous opportunity to advance class mobility and social progress in colonial nations. However, the reality of colonial education has been much less virtuous, since it has been used to oppress and assimilate Indigenous and other marginalized peoples. In addition, the myths of meritocracy and the American dream have distorted the inequitable realities of inequitable educational resources and opportunities. In fact, class mobility has worsened over the last few decades (Chetty et al., 2017, pp. 3–8; Connor & Storper, 2020, pp. 30310–30316), suggesting that very few have been able to leverage education to advance or prosper as suggested by the myth of the American dream (Blume, 2022a, pp. 87–89).

Education in colonial nations has been infused with colonial cultural assumptions. Colonial interpretations of the sciences and humanities are taught. Instruction often focuses on reductionistic perspectives of knowledge that have contributed to compartmentalized and siloed disciplines, artificial boundaries between the human world and the natural world, and artificial distinctions between material and spiritual such that the invisible has been dismissed as less relevant than the visible, measurable world.

Colonial education has perpetuated hierarchical and anthropocentric assumptions about the natural world and the place of humans in it (Blume, 2022b, p. 544). Colonial hierarchies have been used to disempower and minoritize people by defining group superiority and inferiority, justifying colonial privilege and social inequities. Colonial hierarchies have fueled racism and others forms of bias and discrimination that have contributed to separate and unequal educational systems. Hierarchical assumptions in education have contributed to disparities, inequities, and injustices in colonial nations (Blume, 2020, pp. 50–52, 2022a, p. 88).

Colonial education methods have not weathered the COVID-19 pandemic well. The lockdowns and limitations exposed great disparities in educational resources, educational computing and wifi capabilities, educational and mental health capabilities, and safe educational spaces. Furthermore, political divisiveness victimized both students and faculty, resulting in confusing, contradictory, and even risky practices to the health and well-being of staff and students. As a result of these pandemic challenges, educational disparities will likely worsen with time (Blume, 2022a, pp. 89–97). Hierarchical and self-oriented education methods have been insufficient to address the educational challenges. However, it has not been a surprise that educational institutions immersed with cultural values favoring hierarchy, privilege, supremacy, and exceptionalism would contribute to inequitable outcomes, especially during a global crisis. What has been curious, though, is that the colonial educational model founded on assumptions of individualism, autonomy, and self-improvement would fail to prepare students to meet the challenges during a prolonged period of isolation, likely exposing inherent flaws in a self-oriented educational model geared towards autonomy.

An Indigenous worldview does not accept hierarchical assumptions or recognize artificially constructed boundaries that contribute to reductionist views or compartmentalize the spiritual from the material. An Indigenous American perspective acknowledges the centrality and necessity of Creation to its entities, including human creatures, and respects the sacredness and beauty of that Creation and its entities (Blume et al., 2020, pp. 7–12, 2021, pp. 104–105, 2022a, p. 184). An Indigenous worldview emphasizes holism and collectivism—interdependence and kinship rather than independence and autonomy—focusing on the importance of healthy relationships to psychological wellness (Blume, 2020, pp. 88–94). Because of the centrality of Creation over self, an Indigenous American paradigm of psychology assumes that egalitarianism, rather than hierarchies and interdependence, and rather than independence and autonomy, are natural states of being (Blume, 2020, pp. 56). Indigenous education begins with an acceptance of the centrality of Creation as the giver of life and life's lessons, suggesting that instruction begins with the assumption that all entities in Creation are equally sacred, interdependent, and important.

Time in the Western colonial perspective is viewed as linear with a beginning and ending and clear boundaries between past, present, and future (Blume, 2020, pp. 40–42), whereas an Indigenous perspective of time is viewed as cyclical, such that the present has connectivity in the moment with past and future (Blume, 2020, pp. 15–18). Education for human creatures is a life-long cyclical process of becoming—rather than a linear achievement bound to self or siloed from others and the rest of Creation (Blume, 2020, pp. 19–20, 132–133). Education is a holistic and collective enterprise of learning about the sacredness of Creation and its entities—it is destined to be shared with all rather than hoarded by the privileged few for personal gain or profit.

Embracing sacredness is essential for transforming education to benefit all. Imagine how different education would be if participants embraced their collective sacredness and the sacred task of learning from Creation. Imagine how different education would look if egalitarian assumptions regarding curricula, learning, and participants were embraced. Imagine how different an interdependent model of education might look than the current model.

Embracing the sacredness of education may help to overcome the colonial history of exclusion. Colonialism has made educating others seem like a Sisyphean task at times, given colonial inequities of opportunity and resources, colonial linear time demands of deadlines, urgency, and immediacy; and the consequences of years of social inequity and injustice on student preparation. However, an Indigenous conception of cyclical time permits innumerable second chances, which generates patience and hope in the process of intergenerational decolonization and transformation of the social order (Blume, 2020, pp. 96, 101, 171, 227).

Seven daily activities (walks) have been proposed to promote sustainable healing and reconciliation that embraces the sacredness of Creation and its entities (Blume, 2021, pp. 102–108). The seven walks help us think differently about how we educate, develop curricula, generate resources, about the environment in which we educate, and about re-envisioning the relationships of students and teachers. The walks include: 1. the daily educational walk to restore harmony in relationships, 2. the daily educational walk to restore personal balance, 3. the daily educational walk to seek collective beauty, 4. the daily educational walk to advance peace, 5. the daily educational walk to seek humility, 6. the daily educational walk for spiritual centeredness, and 7. the daily educational walk exercising courage.

THE DAILY EDUCATIONAL WALKS TO RESTORE HARMONY IN RELATIONSHIPS AND BALANCE IN SELVES

Teaching harmony and balance as a way of thinking and being embraces collective sacredness. An interdependent and egalitarian existence requires harmony and balance among Creation's entities to thrive. Since colonialism has encouraged hierarchical division, competition, and conflict that has disrupted harmony between human creatures and between the human species and Creation, restoration of harmony with others is essential to psychological wellness, and therefore essential to education. Teaching the importance of harmonious relationships with others in an interdependent egalitarian planetary system would help to embrace sacredness in education.

Seeking moderation is an essential element to restoring personal balance. Moderation requires people to treat oneself with the dignity and respect warranted for a sacred creature. Seeking moderation requires respecting one's physical, mental, emotional, and spiritual well-being, learning to manage time rather than allowing time to manage your existence, and overcoming the imbalances of consumerism and materialism. Embracing personal sacredness restores personal balance from within. Living in a sustainable way restores balances with Creation and with others. Embracing sacredness provides educational clarity on how to tread gently through life, balancing your personal needs with the needs of others across space and time. Embracing sacredness elevates the importance of educating others on seeking both harmony and balance in relationships.

THE DAILY EDUCATIONAL WALKS TO SEEK COLLECTIVE BEAUTY AND ADVANCE PEACE

Seeking collective beauty places one in touch with how sacredness is expressed through Creation's entities. Appreciating the beauty in Creation generates respect for its inherent sacredness—a reminder to treat others with the respect and dignity due to sacred entities. Beauty and awe often go hand in hand when relationships are healthy. Anger, fear, and distrust tend to dim the ability to see beauty, because these emotions interfere with connectivity to the sacredness of Creation (Blume, 2020, pp. 97–98; 2022a, pp. 11, 76–77). Facing the anger, fear, and distrust as an intrapersonal conflict rather than an interpersonal threat will restore one's ability to see the beauty of relationships, but toxic, longstanding externalized anger, fear, and distrust may lead to a dark and lonely place without healing or beauty. It is important to seek restoration from the toxicity by observing daily the collective beauty within us all. Utilizing the beauty of Creation to educate is an important connection to the sacredness of all things.

Every day is an opportunity to seek reconciliation, equity, and advance social and environmental justice in ways that will reduce conflict and promote peace. Hierarchies promote conflict, oppression, violence, and wars in colonial societies. Beliefs in superiority inevitably disrupt the harmony and balances between interdependent and egalitarian creatures. Decolonization involves breaking down the myths of these hierarchies such that they no longer promote inequities and injustices. Teach how hierarchies promote conflict and hinder efforts toward peace in an interdependent and egalitarian planetary order. Teach how seeking healthy relations with others reduces the potential for conflicts and violence.

THE DAILY EDUCATION WALKS TO SEEK HUMILITY AND SPIRITUAL CENTEREDNESS (CREATION-CENTRISM)

Human beings are very small entities in a very large and essentially timeless universe. However, the human capacity for broad and cumulative impact across time is very real, as witnessed by the consequences of climate change (Pörtner et al., 2022, pp. 3–33). Although that impact can result in potentially tragic consequences, it also has the capacity for sustainable and positive outcomes when humans act with the humility required to preserve and advance healthy relationships. The first act of humility, therefore, is acceptance of the reality of an interdependent egalitarian existence. The second act of humility is to develop a keen appreciation for the broad view across space and time of what living in an interdependent and egalitarian existence means—to move beyond colonial hierarchical selfism that has contributed to beliefs that prioritize the needs of this generation and of privileged humans over the rest of Creation. Fully embracing the sacredness of Creation and all of its entities brings about natural humility—one realizes that "us" thinking and "us" behavior is the only logical pathway to harmony, balance, and peace—to find collective beauty in the meaning of one's life.

The daily education walk for spiritual centeredness begins with daily Creation-centric activities to enhance relationships. For Indigenous Peoples, Creation-centrism often is inextricably linked to contact with the natural world. Indigenous people understand the power of restoration and healing available from immersion in nature—a much different perspective than the one that contributes to constructing artificial home, work, and education environments apart from nature. Interestingly, scientists noted that nature was a considerable source of stress relief and healing during the shutdowns of the pandemic (Stock et al., 2022, p. 7), and that buildings well ventilated by outside air were safer than the others (US Environmental Protection Agency, 2022). Schools created in vivo (in nature) will provide higher quality education and promote health and wellness more effectively than the current educational model of constructing artificial environments for learning.

Creation-centric behaviors involve thinking and acting with the big picture in mind, accounting for the impact of one's activities across both space and time. Creation-centrism involves intergenerational thinking and planning—what I have referred to as seven generational living (Blume et al., 2021, pp. 111–112) that simultaneously honors the ancestors and their advances on our behalf and protects those who are yet to come. Seven generational living fosters Creation-centric values, attitudes, beliefs, and actions toward advancing environmental and social justice every day. It involves seeing oneself as part of a larger, evolving whole, and working to honor and learn from the past in order to restore a sustainable future. Creation-centrism accesses the sacred wisdom of the whole to advance collective wellness. Educating people to think collectively across geographic boundaries and generations—to think and problem solve beyond themselves and their cohort—embraces the sacredness of Creation.

Spiritual centeredness helps to foster patience in the unfolding of time in our lives and in our relationships with others, that we are all simultaneously being and becoming throughout of lives until we draw our last breaths. Spiritual centeredness teaches us that we are not in this alone—that there is strength in our collective nature and that time is an ally for change rather than an enemy to be feared. Educating and modeling patience and optimism that trusts in collective sacredness may help to transform lives by changing expectations.

THE DAILY EDUCATIONAL WALK EXERCISING COURAGE

Living in harmony, balance, beauty, peace, humility, and spiritual centeredness takes courage, but walking the other six daily educational walks will access the strengths of Creation to do so. Courage is needed to oppose hierarchies on a daily basis. People of privilege who benefit from those hierarchies may be reluctant to give away the privilege they hold. Courage will be needed to oppose the self-orientation that contributes to the temptations of relational psychopathology (i.e., pursuing self-interests at the expense of others; Blume, 2020, pp. 162–165, 175–178). Self-orientation throws up barriers to healthy relationships and disrupts the daily walks for harmony, balance, beauty, peace, humility, and spiritual-centeredness. Courage is needed to commit daily to the interpersonal activities to remain decolonized. Courage is also necessary to stand against colonial institutions and systems—to call out colonial inequities and injustices that remain infused into hierarchical social systems. Truth to power is needed as the first step to educate for social transformation to prevent future inequities and injustices and to fight the inequities and injustices of the past and present.

The role of warriors in Indigenous societies have been misinterpreted and stereotyped as roles of aggression. In reality, the role of warriors is to defend the peace and protect the vulnerable. Opposing hierarchies, relational psychopathology, selfism, colonialism and its institutions, and standing up for the most vulnerable takes courage. An Indigenous warrior is a defender rather than an offender, operating in a Creation-centric manner (Blume, 2020, pp. 234–235). The role of Indigenous warriors has evolved during colonialism to be agents of decolonization—to challenge privileged self-interests or beliefs of superiority or exceptionalism, and to defend against the violations of Creation-centrism by others.

Decolonizing social systems and institutions takes courage. On a daily basis, those who speak truth to the power of colonization are attacked, berated, blamed, deceived, divided, exploited, manipulated, and even murdered today, just as they have been since the first wave of colonization. Courage is needed to simultaneously stand against these threats and to stand for equity and justice and remain steadfast as a transformative presence. Warrior-educators are needed to encourage others to become allies of decolonization (Blume, 2020, p. 239). Warrior-educators can ensure that sacredness is respected and the vulnerable are provided for and shielded from colonial consequences that hinder learning.

THE SEVEN WALKS PROVIDE AN INDIGENOUS HOLISTIC VISION FOR EDUCATION

The seven walks help to align our individual and collective activities to pro-Creation impact across time and space in order to enhance the psychological wellness of us. Seven generational living reminds educators to be initiators and contributors to transformative processes that will likely remain unfinished in our lifetimes—that in becoming we patiently respect and trust in how the flow of time through its cycles will nourish the seeds of change that educators have planted even if change is invisible to us in the moment of instruction.

Decolonizing education by embracing the sacredness of Creation ensures a legacy of a cadre of students poised to structurally transform societies across the generations. Change may be slow—maybe invisible to us in the moment, with steps forward and sometimes backward, but the cyclical nature of time ensures multiple opportunities for change and provides for patience and hope in the intergenerational process of educating (Blume, 2022b, p. 549). Whole lives will be changed by our instruction, colonial structures will eventually be transformed, and colonial assumptions overturned for an equitable and just future for all.

REFERENCES

Blume, A. W. (2020). *A new psychology based on community, equality, and care of the earth: An indigenous American perspective.* Praeger.

Blume, A. W. (2022a). *Colonialism and the COVID-19 pandemic: Perspectives from indigenous psychology.* Springer Nature.

Blume, A. W. (2022b). Promoting new psychological understandings by use of an indigenous American psychological paradigm. *Journal of Humanistic Psychology, 62*(4), 540–562.

Blume, A. W., Skewes, M. C., & Gardner, S. (2021). *Indigenous Relapse Prevention: Sustaining recovery in Native American Communities.* Cognella.

Chetty, R., Gursky, D., Hell, M., Hendren, N., Manduca, R., & Narang, J. (2017). The Fading American dream: Trends in absolute income mobility since 1940. *Science, 356* (6336), 398–406.

Connor, D. S., & Storper, M. (2020). The changing geography of social mobility in the United States. *PNAS, 117*(48), 30309–30317. https://doi.org/10.1073/pnas.2010222117.

Pörtner, H.-O, Roberts, D. C., Poloczanska, E. S., Mintenbeck, K., Tignor, M., Alegría, A., Craig, M., Langsdorf, S., Löschke, S., Möller, V., & Okem. A. (Eds.). (2022). IPCC, 2022: Summary for policymakers. In *Climate Change 2022: Impacts, Adaptation and Vulnerability. Contribution of Working Group II to the Sixth Assessment Report of the Intergovernmental Panel on Climate Change.* Cambridge: Cambridge University Press.

Stock, S., Bu, F., Fancourt, D., & Mak, H. W. (2022). Longitudinal associations between going outdoors and mental health and wellbeing during a COVID-19 lockdown in the UK. *Scientific Reports, 12*(1). https://doi.org/10.1038/s41598-022-15004-0

US Environmental Protection Agency. (2022). Ventilation and coronavirus (COVID-19). https://www.epa.gov/coronavirus/ventilation-and-coronavirus-COVID-19

CHAPTER 9

IT'S IN OUR DNA!

Holism as an Indigenous Worldview Approach to Happiness

Frank Bracho
Venezuela's Ambassador to India

Frank Bracho offers a convincing case that the concept of happiness has more to do with "being" than with "having" and that the Indigenous proclivity to live in accordance with natural laws is the path toward such personal and communal happiness.

Keywords: Holistic Education, Wellness, Interconnectedness, Indigenous Worldview

I am happy for the invitation to join such distinguished native scholars to speak of "holistic education" from the perspective of Indigenous cosmovisions for a number of six reasons:

1. Education (or, essence-wise, rather: Re-Education) is key to the most pressing task of bringing about an urgent change of consciousness in humanity.

2. Indigenous cosmovision, or worldview, is already in our hearts – in our cultural DNA. (One might think this could make our transformational task much easier.)
3. I know this issue of *HER* is intended to be much more than the worldly career-oriented stuff taught exclusively at "accredited" schools. It has to do with cultural and spiritual values that are "conscientized" at the community-level as a voluntary conviction.
4. It is an opportunity to mirror the ways of beloved Mother Nature.
5. This issue can directly connect us with the most pressing world issues; issues that are a mammoth crisis where modern-day humans have turned their backs on all of nature, including ourselves who are part of it.
6. And finally, I am happy for this chance to write about Indigeneity and holistic thinking because, not by accident, nowadays many people seem curious to turn their eyes to those "Natives" still living according to Nature's laws and are proven and living custodians of Nature's Wisdom that is key to the salvation of the current, magnetic compass-deprived world.

In the past, we have had many notable Indigenous prophetic warnings of what happens when we forget who we are and forget our physical, mental, social, spiritual, and place-based aspects. One ancestor who spoke thusly is Chief Seattle, author of the famous response he addressed to the U.S. President Franklin Pierce in 1855 when the latter intended to "buy" the lands that was the home of Seattle's people. Part of his quote is, "The Earth does not belong to us, we belong to the Earth." Such a sentiment has been echoed from Indigenous wisdom teachings from around the world.

The Hopi, for example, made four visits to the United Nations headquarters in New York to forewarn of the imminent total collapse of the world, the need to "radically change course" and to prepare for a new "Ark of spiritual salvation." The Kogui Mamas of Sierra Nevada of Santa Marta, Colombia procured a BBC documentary, "From the heart of the World: The Elder Brother's Warning," and revealed that human disregard for nature was creating a chain reaction of destruction worldwide. The South African notion of Ubuntu guided such leaders as Nelson Mandela and Archbishop Desmond Tutu toward the interconnect and dignity of interconnected life.

Sadly, these and a plethora of other similar manifestations seem to have fallen on "deaf ears" in the corridors of world power in light of the current ominous, multifaceted global crises we witness all around. On the other hand, it is also fair to say that the sacred and invaluable teachings of Indigenous activists remain "a beacon of light" to a varied, committed, and significant global minority who seem to be listening with the great attention such as those who are reading this journal issue.

So, I write as an Indigenous man with an inescapable duty to speak out with all Indigenous Peoples in these potential "end of times" – who remain the courageous protectors of the last natural wilderness lands of the world. I speak not so much from a scholarly formality, but from a richly experiential common sense, a universal language of the heart. I speak of holistic education as an urgent return to a deep communion with nature that lies in the pre-conquest consciousness of us all. Such consciousness has no skin color, blood type or race. It embodies the physical, mental, social, spiritual and place-based aspects of each of us in ways that are universally interconnected, if only we can nurture each *interdependent* concept. To re-balance life systems, we must be nurtured and guided by actual internalizing experience, not by mere abstract intellectual theoretical notions. How can holistic education via its original manifestation as Indigenous worldview achieve such internalization?

I propose the key is no less and no more than the attainment of happiness. This has always been a fundamental goal, has it not? The pursuit of happiness has been enshrined as a value for nations. Sadly, without the oneness of what Four Arrows and Darcia Narvaez refer to as the kinship worldview, such happiness is elusive and must wrestle with more competitive notions such as wealth. With the kinship worldview, however, the basic needs for happiness emerge. These start with self-actualization from birth, maintained and nurtured with good nutrition, community engagement, parental caring, personal vitality and a feeling of interconnectedness and purpose. In other words, holistic wellness that entwines health with social, mental, spiritual, emotional, and ecological wellness. How can we qualify ancestral Indigenous wisdom in relation to these benchmarks for happiness? However, as we proceed, I suggest that we should not idealize or romanticize Indigeneity. Nor should we deny that they have also been subjected to their own degenerative processes in a cycle that seems to have been inescapable from forced dislocation and a loss of communion with Mother Nature and its laws.

With this in mind, I offer that the term 'happiness' is not explicitly in most Indigenous languages, but lifestyles and attending values did express the concept. The Waraos, the ancestral aborigines of the Orinoco Delta in Venezuela, my homeland, did not have a word for happiness. Rather, they used *"oriwaka"* which has such meanings, depending on context, as waiting together, having a party, joyful sharing with others, and paradise where the dead are happy. Such meanings highlight the importance of sharing of joy and of the transcendent as a key to happiness. In the Piaroa language (a Venezuelan Amazonian ethnic group) happiness is called *"eseusa"* and means "the joy of sharing with others." To the ancient Achaguas Arawak, who also inhabited Venezuela, their word *"chunikai"* meant something more kin to good health or personal vitality.

For the Mayas, the notion of happiness is found in their moral code known as "the Pixab" and says "everything is good as long as it harms no one. I think is right as long as it contributes to the happiness and life at all." In the Maya language Q'eqchi, happiness is called *"sahil ch'oolejil"* and means "having a glad heart," with the word glad probably meaning a combination of healthy, happy oneness with all. Confirming the great centrality that the value of happiness had in

Q'eqchi Mayan life, the main social greeting is *"masa'laa ch'ool,"* which means, "How is your heart?"

The contrast with the European lifestyle serves to raise conscious awareness among Indigenous Peoples about the merits of their ancestral lifestyle relative to happiness. In this regard, the following reflection made around 1676 by Chief Micmac in North America is eloquent: "Which of these is the wisest and happiest, he'll laborers without ceasing and only obtains, with great trouble, enough to live on or he who rest and comfort and finds all he needs on the pleasure of hunting and fishing? There is no Indian who does not consider himself infinitely more happy and powerful than the French" (Nerburn & Mengelkoch, 1991, p. 82). Or, consider Chief Maquinna of the Nootka Nation after he learned about banking practices of the white civilization: "bank, but when we have plenty of money and blankets we give them away to other chiefs and people, and by and by they returned them with interest in our hearts feel good our way of giving is our bank" (Nerburn & Mengelkoch, 1991, p. 82).

Ralph Waldo Emerson, is famous for having said "Our first wealth is our health." I believe it is not a coincidence that he was great friends with Henry David Thoreau whose philosophic work was largely based on Indigenous wisdom (Pratt, 2022). Well-being and optimal social, physical, mental and spiritual fitness was a lifestyle for the traditional American Indian, where in respect and integration with the five elements of the natural order (earth, water, fire, air and ether) was all that was needed for subsistence. Honoring these interconnected elements and their spiritual substance provided good nourishment, housing, clothing, education, exercise, environmental quality, and community-based affection. When one of the facets was out of balance, the Natives would turn to purification ceremonies to recover it. As pointed out in the Maya *Pixab*, when disease, problems, pain and desperation invade our days, it is necessary to perform a purification so that harmony will return, so that peace and happiness will return (Verano & Ubulake, 1993).

Thus, we see that the holistic oneness of earth's five elements and the sense of self, mind, spirit (soul), community and place ultimately are what happiness is all about. This is why an emphasis on materialism in our dominant worldview throws happiness out the window so often. I propose that the most potent explanation for why having or enjoying things does not guarantee happiness is the ephemeral nature of possessions. Those who are attached are destined to suffer when possessions disappear as inevitably, they must be removed from our lives. This is why Indigenous Peoples do not understand the dominant culture's strong attachments to objects. Although personal vitality for living on earth is important, the Indigenous holistic perspective also realizes that too much attachment to our bodies and fear of death stifles authentic happiness. It is separation from the oneness of all, the Natural Order, that is the enemy of happiness. To reach happiness we need to recognize that being is linked to the transcendent. Ancestral Indigenous wisdom understands integration with Creation and the Natural Order is most conducive to happiness.

I close by saying happiness is a vital life mission on our beautiful planet. It is dependent upon alignment with our natural identity and sense of a deep sense of interconnectedness with nature, a phenomenon of which we are part (despite the dictionary definitions that say otherwise). Happiness is having a fearless heart that recognizes the significance of all life, including our own, no matter what artificial designs a civilization imposes. Such impositions from the dominant cultures that over-emphasize the dominant anthropocentric, materialist fear-based worldview, have corrupted the true way to happiness. With each species that becomes extinct, each river that becomes polluted, child that goes unwanted, conflict that ignores the laws of Mother Nature, we each lose some of ourselves, with happiness being the first to go. The return, however, is easy, because our interconnectedness with the cosmos is in our DNA!

REFERENCES

Nerburn, K., & Mengelkoch, L. (1991). *Native American wisdom.* New World Library.

Pratt, S. L. (2022). Lessons in place: Thoreau and indigenous philosophy. *Metaphilosophy, 53*(4). https://doi.org/10.1111/meta.12563.

Verano, J., & Ubulake, D. (1993). *Seeds of change: Readers on cultural exchange after 1492.* Addison-Wesley.

CHAPTER 10

PROVEN SUSTAINABLE TEACHINGS FROM INDIGENOUS AND MAROON PEOPLES

A Model for Holistic Educators

Sox Sperry

Ithaca College, Ithaca, NY; Center for Nonviolence, Fort Wayne, IN

This article explores the author's journey as the founder and curator of Proven Sustainable, a website that shares the voices of Indigenous and Maroon cultures that have managed to live sustainably for hundreds of years. It reveals how this journey and the nature-based Indigenous teachings of the website it led to are an ultimate example of holistic education that should be part of every classroom.

Keywords: Indigeneity, Indigenous Peoples, Decolonization, Educational Resource

As a young white boy growing up in suburban New Jersey in the 1960s, my media-influenced view of possible futures was informed mostly by the Jetsons and Star Trek. These futures were led by white men who saw high-tech engineering as the path to the promised land. Then, when I was 20, I spent five months as a student teacher at Taos Pueblo Day School. Standing beneath the sacred Taos Mountain at recess, I found my mentors in two Taosena teachers, Tonita Lujan and Crucita Archuleta. From that vantage point beneath Pueblo Peak, the future looked much like the past—steady state community life informed by ancient enduring traditions fixed squarely on sacred land.

Fifty years later popular media representations of the future haven't changed that much with Elon Musk and Jeff Bezos seeking to colonize space and fossil fuel giant BP changing its name to Beyond Petroleum. Like George Jetson and Captain Kirk, we once again see white men selling techno-futures only now with a green label. But Taos Pueblo represents a sustainable future by keeping faith with the past on land they've fought to protect ever since the Pueblo Revolt of 1680.

For the past 20 years, I've worked as the main curriculum writer for Project Look Sharp, an educational program based at Ithaca College that promotes media and digital literacy. In 2011, we published a collection of lessons entitled, "Media Constructions of Sustainability: Food, Water and Agriculture," the first of a series of such collections devoted to encouraging students to think critically about what sustainability means and how sustainability interweaves with social justice. As I researched media documents that would help to unearth these themes, I became frustrated by the lack of mainstream attention to the traditions of people whose very survival in the face of the assaults of nation states should be recognized as proof that sustainable culture is possible.

I began to look for examples of such "proven sustainable" cultures and realized that there are Indigenous Peoples across the globe who have held their ground as much as the people of Taos Pueblo have, for a very long time. I also found myself drawn to the experiences of the Maroon—freedom fighters of African descent in the Americas, who steadfastly demonstrate sustained freedom in place across the centuries of resistance to enslavement and white supremacy. These indomitable Indigenous and Maroon freedom fighters represent dynamic and resilient cultures that, in the words of Seneca activist and scholar John Mohawk, understand "humankind's relationship to nature (through a) pre-colonial, pre-patriarchal, pre-modern story." If I want to imagine what a just, free and sustainable future might look like I turn my face to their examples as offered on our Proven Sustainable website.

As my independent study advisor, Jim Koplin read my early writings about my desire to teach, he recognized and named a key truth that I needed to acknowledge and work within a disciplined manner: "You see things in a really culture-bound way. It's probably true that most people on this globe live in circumstances where all of the things that you (and I) worry about could not possibly make any difference." I was humbled and awakened. Jim became a friend and mentor throughout the rest of his life. He introduced me to Dr. Gloria Joseph, through whose class I managed to arrange my student teaching on Taos Pueblo. Gloria also became a lifelong friend and (her word) "womentor." Forty years later, from her bedside in

St Croix, she sent me to pick a healing stone from Maroon Ridge for her healing altar.

Gloria was the first person with whom I discussed my seed thoughts for Proven Sustainable. I told her I wanted to learn with and support people who have demonstrated genuine sustainability beliefs and practices across the planet for hundreds of years. She said, "We know that sustainability relies not on technology but on relationships—to one another, all creatures and the living earth. Your understanding of 'the sacred' is critical." She pointed to her portrait of Chief Joseph with the quote, "The earth and myself are of one mind." She went on, "The phrase 'Nothing is sacred' means that the truly sacred has been damaged by the forces of empire, along with the very meaning of the word 'sacred.' Your goal is to point back to that which was rendered invisible without using the language of the systems that damaged sacredness."

Through my relationship with Gloria, I realized that the only way to "honor the sacred" was to offer the words of people who have lived the very beliefs and practices, which can help us to remember what it means to be a human being existing in relationship to a living earth. I knew that I needed to be expansive in my offering of voices. I selected *Proven Enduring* peoples who have lived in place for 500 years or longer, stewarding and defending their land while making no efforts to colonize distant peoples: the Khomani San and Hadza from Africa, the Yolngu and Noongar from Australia, the Zhongnan Mountain hermits and Ainu from Asia, the Sami and Basque from Europe, the Chukchi and Inuit from the Arctic, the Haudenosaunee and Hopi from North America, the Kogi and Quechua from South America, the Hawaiians and Maori from Oceania. For the *Proven Free* assemblies, I identified peoples of African descent who have lived in place for 150 years or longer in the Caribbean and the Americas, stewarding their African roots and defending their land against white supremacy: the Saamaka Maroons and Quimbolas from South America, the Haitian Vodouists and Jamaican Maroons from the Caribbean, the Gullah Geechee and Black Seminoles from North America.

Through online research I sought the words of women, men, and two spirit people, young and old, in traditional community and in diaspora. For each of these 22 assemblies I found the words of eight people, 176 voices in total. Each individual on the Proven Sustainable website is represented by a dialogue code, a quotation of theirs and an accompanying image along with questions intended to inspire collective reflection and action about how we might sustain ourselves on a living planet. As I shared this project with others, Ketu named the need to ask permission of all those represented on the Proven Sustainable website. As he said, "In life, relationship is everything and it begins with I am. Not the 'I am black, and you are white' of American race relations. But the humanity that connects us. From the common 'I am' I see that You are."

Then began the lengthy process of tracking down addresses for as many of the individuals as I could and mailing each a letter letting them know that I hoped to repost their words and inviting their response and participation in collective decision-making and collaborative creativity.

I wrote to them about the intended readers and purposes for this project:

1. Members of Proven Sustainable communities to extend and reinforce bridges to other traditional Peoples and to connect with non-traditional individuals whom they might want to educate and from whom they might want to solicit material aid and support.
2. Young people with cultural roots in proven sustainable communities to extend education about their own traditions and to make them aware of beliefs and practices of other traditional Peoples.
3. Community educators in non-Indigenous communities to initiate discussion and action in support of cultural change in the world toward Proven Sustainable beliefs and practices.

I also wrote that the Proven Sustainable website would not accept donations or allow advertisements but instead encourage readers to make direct donations to support projects identified by the Peoples represented on the Proven Sustainable website. A majority of those who replied were supportive of the project. A small number requested that I remove their codes, which we did right away. Several of those who replied agreed to participate in our Proven Sustainable Conversations Series led by lead interviewer Ketu Oladuwa and website designer and Conversation Series director Kelsey Greene. These are videotaped discussions with Indigenous and Maroon Peoples and their supporters intended to realize and challenge our conscious and unconscious colonized thinking and behaviors in order to better inform our actions amidst challenging situations we face worldwide. Each conversation explores individual and cultural beliefs and practices for living sustainably and resiliently amidst drastic environment changes and ongoing historical efforts of erasure.

Two of the Proven Sustainable Conversation participants, Nicole McIntosh and Wahinkpe Topa (Four Arrows), agreed to become members of the Proven Sustainable guiding council, which aims to shepherd the development of the Proven Sustainable Conversation Series through sincere relationship-building efforts.

Their essential words help to underscore and actualize the goals of our work with Proven Sustainable. I borrow their words with gratitude to close this writing:

Nicole McIntosh, proud Jamaican Maroon: "The legacy that you are creating with this platform is really, really important for us as we go through life and learn about other cultures. You know when I come to your platform I'm thinking, 'Well I've never heard of this—all the Maroons there. It's just wonderful.' I click the button and I navigate, and I'm excited like a child when I'm on that platform."

Wahinkpe Topa (Four Arrows), professor in the School of Leadership Studies at Fielding Graduate University: "As educators use decolonization to challenge educational and cultural hegemony, we must also replace it with Indigenous perspectives and values that guided us for most of human history in ways that cultivate more peaceful, healthy and happy relationships in and with the world."

Nicole and Four Arrows bring me back to where I started. To the centrality of relationship-building as a means to stand in solidarity with and for the indomitable survivors who are honored on this website.

CHAPTER 11

RECOVERING THE SPIRIT, BONE BY BONE

Colonization and the Classroom

Amba J. Sepie
Massey University, Aotearoa, NZ

This paper considers the loss of Spirit, as linked to a sentient view of Earth, alongside the issue of colonization as a cultural mode, a worldview, and a chimeric, yet often invisible player in our classrooms. Following the work of Four Arrows and the kinship value structure inherent in the cosmologies and practice of Earth-oriented Indigenous and Traditional communities across time and geographies, I offer a series of observations and adjustments to how we might collectively proceed with the work of holistic education with a Spirit-Earth focus and an eye on the constant presence of colonized consciousness.

Keywords: Mixed Heritage, Colonization, Fifth World, Ancestral Memory, Indigenous Communities

As we approach what is variously called the Fifth World, the Sixth Sun, the Great Turning, and so on, we are being called to recalibrate our relationship with Earth and Spirit. And yes—I am citing prophecy. Without Spirit, the very essence of which has been exorcised from both culture and classroom, no real decolonization is possible. Without Spirit, we are but hollow bones on a spinning rock: fragile, brittle, and easily broken.

I write this as a woman of mixed heritage and mixed influence: neither this, nor that. I was born already colonized, as are many of us, and have had to dream a track back to the relationships that are both birthright and lived responsibility. I have come to know intuition as separate from the voices in my mind. I have come to listen more closely to Earth speaking her guidance. And through the practice of transmission, attempted to awaken in others the realization that we can never be disconnected from those forces that sustain us. As a teacher in the classroom, however, I have also come to realize that there is always an invisible presence sitting with us as we learn, and her name is Trauma. She carries a secret we have collectively learned to silence, suppress, and deny – that regardless of historical context, and separate from ethnicity, we are all, at multiple levels, colonized.

To suggest that we have all been colonized out of our relationship with Earth and Spirit, is, in these times, a radical statement. And yet – there it is, with an emphasis on the word 'all.'[1] We are accustomed to considering this word *colonization* to be linked only with the struggles of Indigenous communities against the forces of empire over the last five hundred years. In this moment of our time, however, these same mechanisms continue to operate through modernization, globalization, capitalist expansion, and ideological deceit. The poverty trap forces accelerated colonization for some, the illusion of progress forces others, and for many, extended isolation from necessary sustainable and local resources, and a grounded culture, has given humans no option but to comply. The juggernaut of the colonizing worldview pushes ever onward as an assimilative, destructive, absorptive engine that is now so prolific its continuance seems permanent. And yet common sense would tell us that it was not always this way.

As John Mohawk and the Haudenosaunee argued, in 1978:

> The traditional Native peoples hold the key to the reversal of the processes in Western Civilization which hold the promise of unimaginable future suffering and destruction. Spiritualism is the highest form of political consciousness. And we, the native peoples of the Western Hemisphere, are among the world's surviving proprietors of that kind of consciousness. We are here to impart that message. (Mohawk, 2005, pp. 90–91)

But as it is now 2023, it would appear this 45-year-old message is yet to 'settle upon' the rest of Earth's people. Without the acknowledgment of Spirit, without accepting this invitation, we remain largely unable to fulfill our responsibilities as humans to Earth.

---

[1] I am by no means the first to point in this direction. See the following authors: Mohawk (1978); Jackson (2007); Donald (2010); Curry (2010); Parry, (2015).

If we draw upon Four Arrows' work on the criticality of worldview for our educational work, we can align this state of colonization with the dominant worldview and trace its influence back through time. We can expand upon it progressively, for in every classroom, family, village, town, city, and country, and on every limb of Earth, everywhere and for everyone, the colonizing or dominant worldview is in some way *active* and impacting our relationships. For those who identify as settler, modern, or of pan-European descent, this can appear as an unremembered and unacknowledged influence, especially if the forcible removal of ancestors from place in the ancient establishment of city states is inaccessible to memory. And yet there *was* a process by which the colonized became the colonizer, and thus became absorbed into the cultural complex of mobile and acquisitional forces, acting under Kingship or Chiefdoms, in pursuit of resource theft by elimination and occupation.[2] Logically, the ancestors of all humans maintained close relationships with places, but not all have maintained their Indigeneity. Understanding how this happened and what it has created can unlock grief from the inherited identities of our forebears in a manner that dissolves some of the polarities and divisions carried forward into the present day.

There is a set of definitions that can guide us. First, the central difference between colonization and colonialism is that, whilst Indigenous peoples possess a *living* ancestral memory of the collective losses wrought by colonialism and can make concrete connections between colonial violences and cultural and physical losses, those who were colonized by processes prior to living ancestral memory *do not*. We can locate colonialism in a continuum with colonization, but the latter stretches back much further into deep time. The difference is temporal.

Colonizing processes can be identified primarily as possessing a logic of replacement, assimilation, and ultimately, absorption of local places and peoples into a conglomerate, nation, or city-state, for the purposes of either human resources (labor) or natural resources (land, minerals, etc.). The mechanisms of control included, as a fundamental feature, the systematic and deliberate replacement of worldview at the level of religion and ritual practice, and the severing of relational, familial, geographical, and community bonds, as generally accompanied by the threat of violence or death. Early colonization processes were continued, generation after generation, to eventually manifest as the colonialism we *do* all remember, perpetuated by those who were colonized before memory.

Trauma, and the extreme fragmentation of our understanding of Earth and Spirit, has been the result. In the words of Jon Young, the historic trauma that caused Western societies to develop this amnesia has created the most discon-

---

[2] To frame the colonizers as formerly colonized is not to adopt an apologist stance regarding the continuance of colonialism across the world (into contemporary times), as perpetuated by successive governments, institutions, and communities in ways which show absolutely no respect for Indigenous peoples, nor aid recovery from colonial violences. Rather, I am emphasizing that the behaviors of those who initiated, and continue, the colonial project, have a history that goes beyond contemporary settler-colonial academic discourses.

nected active social system on the planet (Young, 2015). The remedy, I believe, is to begin to teach with *compassion* toward those humans who are in a state of being whereby the original trauma has been forgotten.

I like to think of this state as similar to having charcoal on our hands, a metaphor I believe I am borrowing from a half-recollected talk by Robin Wall Kimmerer.[3] We know about charcoal, we can visualize this well, we can understand how it can get on everything. Now imagine the charcoal is invisible, creating black marks we cannot see.[4] This is how it is when we remain in a state of denial, or fail to bring these ideas into the classroom. Cultural design for education needs to include some awareness of what is active in the psyche of students regarding fear, belief, and control – an inherited set of conditioning parameters on the expression of their being that is generally unconscious. As written in a recent memoir by Stephanie Foo, and this resonates so powerfully with what I witness in the classroom: "Every cell in my body is filled with the code of generations of trauma, of death, of birth, of migration, of history that I cannot understand… I want to have words for what my bones know" (Foo, 2022, p. 202).

So it is, with care, that we might decide to name this invisible presence and see how it blocks connection, awareness, and understanding. To follow along the lines argued by religious scholar Suhayb Yunus, there needs to be a kind of *ketosis*, or emptying out, of the colonized precepts that are living silently within us (Yunus, 2021).

If we wish to secure a future in which the traditional values of Indigenous peoples become the guidelines for human experience, we must attend to those invisible masters, irrespective of the timeline within which ancestral colonization occurred. In my own teaching practice, I draw upon history, geography, anthropology, neuroscience, physiology, and studies of religion and race to expose the long-term exorcism wrought by these colonizing processes, not to indoctrinate students into any particular view of Spirit, but to demonstrate the manner in which Spirit has been reshaped, suppressed, or recharacterized to comply with very human agendas.[5]

I present Earth as sentient and possessing of a consciousness to which we are all internal. We learn about custodial practices toward other species and the wider ecologies within which we are enmeshed. I profile a steady flow of wisdom drawn from Indigenous lifeways and living value systems (consistent across all Earth-oriented communities, across time, and across the body of Earth), and walk with students as we explore different ideas about Earth, consciousness and ecologies. I

---

[3] If I may direct you to her book instead, Kimmerer (2013).

[4] As echoed in these words by Brian Kim, "every step that I take towards decoloniality is tempered by the very coloniality of my existence." Brian Kim (2021).

[5] Key here is the definition of two cultural strands, Earth-oriented and War-oriented, that can be shown to manifest in the form of the circle, and the pyramid, thus depersonalizing some of the most difficult aspects of worldview transformation by de-coupling the two cultural forces from specific groups of people in order to examine them objectively.

explain the symbolic architecture of different communities in a non-appropriative way, in order to demonstrate that there are many paths that can spiral out from very similar value systems, and that the value system itself is not culturally dependent. In short, we *accept the invitation* to become students of Earth, directly; to become apprenticed to Indigenous value systems as consistent models of correct socioecological conduct; and, to agree to do the work of decolonizing ourselves – as a human group – in a heart-centered and grounded way that sees and attends to the presence of trauma with a focus on healing those aspects of ourselves that have been denied.

Surely, we have no more time for debate. Davi Kopenawa, of the Yanomamö, reminds us that when humans forget our proper function and cease to serve life, the world falls apart (Kopenawa & Albert, 2013). This is where we are, in an exorcised world on the verge of the next one. Unprepared. Yet surrounded by advisors, those Elders who speak out, those ancestors whose words have been recorded or remembered, and those voices that emanate from the world of information, existing just out of sight, behind the veil.

Across time, and beyond our own small identities, if we can only reach far enough into the deep memories of Earth, we *know* what we are. When we place our bare feet on the body of Earth and we feel the web beneath us, holding us in her consciousness and drawing us into her. We know we have roots there. We know what we are and that we belong to a story that is much older than we may consciously realize. And so it is with care, that we might be conduits to reclaim and release the life songs and knowing from the once hollow bones of our brothers, sisters, others, and beloved kin, into the air, once again.

REFERENCES

Curry, P. (2010). Some remarks on Val Plumwood. *Green Letters, 12*(1), 8–14.

Donald, D. (2010). On what terms can we speak? Aboriginal-Canadian relations as a curricular and pedagogical imperative. In *Big Thinking lecture series for the Congress of the Humanities and Social Sciences*. University of Lethbridge.

Foo, S. (2022). *What my bones know: A memoir of healing from complex trauma*. Ballantine Books.

Jackson, M. (2007). Globalisation and the colonising state of mind. In M. Bargh (Ed.), *Resistance: An indigenous response to neoliberalism* (pp. 167–82). Huia.

Kim, B. (2021). *Debriefing on decoloniality—A public conversation*, Part 2. https://jcrt.org/religioustheory/2021/06/22/debriefing-on-decoloniality-a-public-conversation-part-2/.

Kimmerer, R. W. (2013). *Braiding sweetgrass: Indigenous wisdom, scientific knowledge and the teachings of plants*. Milkweed Editions.

Kopenawa, D., & Albert, B. (2013). *The falling sky: Words of a Yanomami Shaman*. Belknap Press of Harvard University Press.

Mohawk, J. (Ed.). (2005). *Basic call to consciousness*. Akwesasne Notes/Book Publishing Company, 1978. Reprint, 2005.

Parry, G. A. (2015). *Original thinking: A radical revisioning of time, humanity, and nature.* North Atlantic Books.

Young, J. (2015). Going forth with active hope: Deep nature connection, mentoring and culture repair. In *Bioneers resilient communities network event*. UC Santa Cruz.

Yunus, S. (2021). *Debriefing on decoloniality—A public conversation, Part 1.* https://thenewpolis.com/(2021)/06/15/debriefing-on-decoloniality-a-public-conversation/.

CHAPTER 12

I LIVE HERE

Shannon Kenny
Prontopia (Alliloop.io), Santa Barbara, CA

A poem of place, connection, and identity.

Keywords: Nature, Indigenous Poetry, Family, Indigenous Stories

Where do I live?

I live where the raindrops fall, where the scent of jasmine fills me up.
I live where the gentle night tide whispers on golden sands,
in the seamless seas that unite us all.

I live on the back of a silvery steed with kind, knowing eyes.
Inhabiting ancient stories.
I live in wonder. I live in history.

I live in my lover's strong embrace and my daughters' smiles.
In a mother's song, a father's words, a brother's admiration.
I live in laughter among friends, where I'm dancing.

I live in a silence that is sometimes broken by graceful doves taking flight.
And where ancestors whisper through the sweetgrass.

In the shade of a tangled olive tree, waiting for peace.

I live on a winding road marked by wise oak trees—gatekeepers to my dreams.
My heart is my home,
I live here.

CHAPTER 13

LIVING HOLISTICALLY

Practicing the Navajo Principles of *Hózhǫ́* and *K'é*

Miranda Jensen Haskie
Diné College, Tsaile, AZ

In this article the author introduces the Navajo (Diné) principles of Hózhǫ́ and K'é as a foundation for holistic learning and living. She tells how her grandfather's life represented these principles and how he manifested them in the world. She shows how his model reveals that holistic education is about living holistically as was foundational to Indigenous cultures prior to colonization. She offers her grandfather's way of being as a model for holistic living.

Keywords: Navajo, Indigenous worldview, Chic Sandoval, Indigenous Education, Holistic Living, Family

DINÉ SELF-INTRODUCTION

Yá'át'ééh Diné Shik'éí, I am *Diné* of the *'Áshįįhí* (Salt clan), born for *Tł'ízí Łání* (Many Goats clan), my maternal grandfather is *Kin Łichíi'nii* (Red house clan) and my paternal grandfather is *Tó Dích'íi'nii* (Bitterwater clan). Miranda Jensen Haskie *yinishyé* (my name). I am from Lukachukai, Arizona on the Navajo

Nation. I was raised at a time when western education was encouraged and the completion of a college degree was expected in my family since both my father and mother completed their bachelor's degrees. However, to attain and complete the western education, it meant I had to leave home – my home among the four sacred mountains. I spent my junior high and most of my high school years attending school on the Navajo Nation. I spent my senior year of high school and my undergraduate years off the Navajo Nation in western schools.

In time, I realized everything I needed to succeed was inherent in my Navajo culture; yet, the colonizing educational experience led me to believe otherwise. The colonizing perspective soon had me view my world from a linear approach. In western education, I was trained to complete my formal education according to this linear model. While away, I constantly longed to return home; with the support of *shimásání* (my grandmother), uncles and sisters, I remained in Albuquerque, New Mexico to complete my bachelor's degree. Upon completing my Bachelor of Arts in Sociology from the University of New Mexico, I returned home to Lukachukai, Arizona. Now that I was home, I had no desire to ever leave home again, but I knew I wanted to eventually earn a graduate degree. I wondered whether an accredited graduate degree program was available to me without leaving home.

Fielding Graduate University was the graduate school that allowed me to continue in my career at Diné College while pursuing a Doctorate in Educational Leadership and Change. The faculty and curriculum at Fielding were unique in that I was encouraged to apply my indigenous worldview in my doctoral studies. For my dissertation, I conducted a grounded theory research study on the life of my grandfather, *Shicheii*, Albert "Chic" Sandoval, Sr. (1892–1968). I respectfully refer to him as *Shicheii* or by his nick-name, Chic, throughout this writing.

Chic lived in the early 20th century and was an accomplished interpreter and translator of the Navajo language. He lived and worked to preserve our culture, practicing the Navajo principles of *Hózhǫ́* and *K'é*. *Hózhǫ́* is the Navajo principle of beauty and striving for harmony and balance. As Diné people, we continually strive to practice and achieve *Hózhǫ́* daily. *K'é* is the Navajo principle of establishing and maintaining relationship with all in our environment.

Many Diné people continue to practice *K'é* daily. It is an all-encompassing practice that pervades every aspect of Diné daily life. These Diné principles have been practiced time immemorial and remain as valuable today as they were historically. In this article, I discuss how *Shicheii* lived holistically practicing the Navajo principles of *Hózhǫ́* and *K'é*. This practice can be important for all Diné educators, education administrators, and students.

The Navajo Basket symbolizes living holistically and offers a way for educators to teach *Hózhǫ́* and *K'é* (harmony, balance, and good relationships with all). It represents the holistic connection of people in multiple ways as taught in centuries-old Navajo tradition. It has many interpretations. One relates to the interconnectedness between self, family, community, culture, nation, and universe.

- **Self**—living the Navajo Principles of *Hózhǫ́* and *K'é* (live in harmony and establish a relationship with oneself) including that of knowing oneself at many levels (emotionally, intellectually, spiritually, and socially)
- **Family**—practicing the principles with family (nuclear, extended, and clan family)
- **Community**—living in harmony and establishing a relationship with those in the community where the individual resides (local level)
- **Culture**—living in harmony and establishing a relationship with members of the same ethnic or cultural group (for example, Navajo)
- **Nation**—living in harmony and establishing a relationship with the nation in which the individual resides (from the Navajo Nation to the United States, U.S. being the nation)
- **Universe**—living in harmony and establishing a relationship with mother earth, father sky, and natural elements in our environment (continuous; ongoing)

My grandfather, Chic, practiced *Hózhǫ́* and *K'é* to live holistically as it relates to each of these. Commencing with the *self*, he learned to live in harmony by coming to know himself emotionally, intellectually, spiritually, and socially. From this, he was able to practice *Hózhǫ́* and *K'é* with *family*. Family comprised his nuclear family, extended family, and clan relatives. Clan relatives in the Navajo culture refers to those relatives a Navajo is related to by Navajo clanship. The Navajo people exercise clanship in relationship with each other. The Diné people engage in a highly sophisticated application of establishing clan relationship with one another. *Hak'éí* is relative by blood or clanship (Young & Morgan, 1987). Chic's maternal clan was *Kin Łichíi'nii* (Red House clan). To demonstrate the complex system of Navajo kinship, the clan relatives of the *Kin Łichíi'nii* (Red House clan) include *Deeshchii'nii* (Start of the Red Streak clan), *Tł'ízí Łání* (Many Goats clan), *Tł'ááshchí'í* (Red Bottom People clan), *Tsé nahabiłnii* (Sleep Rock People clan), *Tsi'naajinii* (Black Streak Wood People clan), and *Naashashí* (Bear People clan) (Young & Morgan, 1987).

Owing to Chic's ability to live according to *Hózhǫ́* and *K'é*, he eventually became a cultural intermediary and a vanguard for his people. This relates to the *community* stage. The practice of the Navajo principles, the language, and his work as an interpreter and translator, helped him preserve the Navajo *culture* on behalf of the Navajo Nation, the *nation*. He did this while maintaining an intimate and harmonious relationship with the *universe*, *Nahasdzáán Shimá* (mother earth) and *Yádiłhił Shitaa'* (father sky).

Chic's modeling and teaching about living in balance in each domain inspired others to do so (Haskie, 2002). At the first level the *self*, he was generous and kind. He was always willing to help anybody that asked him. In level two, Chic demonstrated an uncompromising commitment to *family*, often attending ceremonies for helping relatives. Relating to level four, *culture*, he valued *Hózhǫ́* and encouraged his cultural practices. This sense of culture also inspired Navajo government which leads to his engagement at level five of *K'é*, the *nation*, Chic had many good friends throughout the Navajo nation and treated everyone as members of the Tribe. He often brought gifts such as mutton and returned home with presents like bread or pottery.

Chic's prayers speak to level six of *K'é*, *universe*. He understood the importance of the *Diyin* and the wonder of the universe. He knew the interconnection about the importance of reciprocity on Earth applied throughout the cosmos.

Thus, living holistically by practicing the principles of *Hózhǫ* and *K'é* is that we realize that the individual is inseparable from the universe and everything in it. At the same time, it embraces the beauty all around no matter the difficulties one encounters. Chic, my revered grandfather, was a model for such holistic living and never stopped seeing the beauty in others and inspired others to see the beauty in themselves.

- *Shitsijį' hózhǫǫ doo*
- *Shikéédę́ę́' hózhǫǫ doo*
- *Shiyaagi hózhǫ doo*
- *Shik'igi hózhǫǫ doo*
- *Shinaagi hózhǫǫ doo*
- *Shizaad hahóózhǫǫ doo*
- *Sa'ąh Naagháí Bik'eh Hózhǫ́ Nishłį́į́ doo*

English Version

- Let there be blessing before me
- Let there be blessing behind me
- Let there be blessing below me
- Let there be blessing above me
- Let there be blessing all around me
- Let there be blessing through the words I speak
- I have become one with the spirit, I am what the spirit wants of me.
- Let there be blessing (Office of Diné Culture, Language & Community Services, 2000)

REFERENCES

Haskie, M. J. (2002). *Preserving a culture: Practicing the Navajo principles of Hozho doo K'é*. Doctoral dissertation. Fielding Graduate University.

Office of Diné Culture, Language & Community Services. (2000). *T'áá Shá Bik'ehgo Diné Bí Ná nitin dóó Íhoo'aah*. Division of Diné Education.

Young, R. W., & Morgan, W. (1987). *The Navajo language dictionary*. University of New Mexico Press.

CHAPTER 14

LEARNING TO WALK RELATIONALLY AND LIVE MÉTIS

Jennifer Markides
University of Calgary, AB, Canada

Métis is a complex identity, both born out of and shaped by the history of colonization in Canada. Despite playing essential roles in ensuring the survival of early settlers and working as mediators between Indigenous and Settler peoples to present day, Métis have been marginalized and misunderstood for centuries. Yet, somehow, we thrive. In this chapter, Jennifer shares her experiences as a Métis person, learning about and living our worldview that centres relationships and accountability to others. She expresses gratitude to her teachers who have helped her to view the world differently, through ceremony and fostering her relationship to place.

Keywords: Métis, Relationships, Responsibilities, Community, Interconnectedness, Place-Based, Spirituality.

Returning to what is customary in many Indigenous circles, I will begin by introducing myself. The practice is similar to stating one's positioning in a research paper, but with an emphasis on the relationships that connect us to specific families, communities, locations, ontologies, epistemologies, and worldviews, in what

Kathy Absolon and Cam Willett describe as putting ourselves forward (2005, p. 97). In Métis gatherings, family names are often repeated by others; we share our community connections as a way of making kin. In doing so, we are also establishing trust, because our families and communities hold us accountable to each other.

Respectfully, I offer that I am Métis with family ties to Red River. Beginning in the 19th century, my family members moved west and north across Canada, some even followed other Métis kin south into Seattle, Washington. My family names are McKay (John Richards), Favel, Ballendine, Linklater, and McDermott. I was raised in unceded Wet'suwet'en territory in northern British Columbia on land that borders the unceded territory of the Gitxsan. From an early age, I knew I was Indigenous, but like many, I did not have a clear idea of what that meant. My lack of understanding did not stop me from claiming and celebrating my indigeneity throughout school. When we would discuss heritage and culture in class, I would announce it proudly even if I was met by jeers, disbelief, or an exacerbated teacher—like Leanne Betasamosake Simpson encountered during her grade 3 class trip to the sugar bush (2014, p. 6). Because why would anyone want to identify or associate as a primitive or lesser being? Fortunately, I was naïve to the racism and had the privilege of growing up surrounded by family, both Métis and Settler, inclusive of Swedish and English grandparents on my mom's side. For over twenty-five years I have been learning what it means to be Métis: first, by respecting my grandpa's troubled relationship with being Indigenous, then connecting with teachers and seeking out spaces of Métis community.

Métis are often described as walking in two worlds, but rarely with the recognition and respect for who Métis are as a distinct people (LaRocque, forthcoming). Social studies, history textbooks, and educators have described Métis people as having been born of unions between primarily French or English fur traders who had taken Indigenous wives during the earliest days of colonization. Known as "half-breeds" and mixed-blood, Métis warranted their own supervisory agency. This was the North West Half-Breed Commission run by the Department of the Interior in the early years of Canada. There are many misconceptions of who the Métis are, so it's no wonder people are claiming Métis when they learn about a distant Indigenous relative. People tended to not question *Métis-ness* out of politeness, disinterest, ignorance, or apathy. Métis have only recently been recognized as a distinct Indigenous group in Canada *(Daniels v. Canada,* 2016, SCC 12). Identifying as Métis requires a connection to the early Métis people and communities typically associated with Red River and the development of commerce, distinct language (Michif) and ways of living (Shore, 2018, p. 16)

For a long time, Métis have been treated as second class Indigenous citizens (Lavallee, forthcoming); it could be argued that we continue to be discriminated against as not Indigenous or not Indigenous enough and that doesn't say much for the treatment of Métis because Indigenous people have been billed as primitive, lesser beings who have needed to be saved and civilized through acts of colonization (King, 2003, p. 131).

Legacies of colonization have made Indigenous identity a precarious landscape to navigate as people have been forcibly disconnected from their communities through residential school systems, the 60s Scoop, the child welfare system, and internalized shame that has been passed down from generation to generation, to name a few (Markides, 2021, p. 108). People have chosen to not teach their children and grandchildren the language or spiritual teachings that might bring them harm or hardship for *being* Indigenous (St. Denis, 2007, pp. 1073–1077).

Beyond the Indian Act and other oppressive policies, hegemonic societal structures have continued to perpetuate ignorance and stereotypes of the "noble savage" and untamed lands free for the taking (King, 2003, p. 78; Williams, 2021, p. 25). Western education has taught the narratives of colonization and continues to colonize through schooling that is biased and partial, privileging the stories that support and reify the dominant worldview.

Like many Indigenous people who have been educated in the public-school systems, we are having to decolonize our minds, bodies, and spirits to unlearn and relearn the teachings of our Elders and ancestors. The opportunities to reclaim knowledge and learn through ceremony are gifts to all of us. These experiences are often life changing.

The processes and paths back to our communities, knowledges, and ways of being are varied. Sometimes the events that lead us back to community are tumultuous and involve great personal losses. Racism still exists in society and in the subsequent social systems such as health care, justice, education, and child welfare. Despite the structure and barriers that have created distrust and inequity, First Nations, Métis, and Inuit people have survived many forms of genocide—past and present. Our strength, resilience, and hope come from our kinship circles.

On my personal journey of Indigenous education, I have been fortunate to have had opportunities to learn from Cree, Métis, and Anishinaabe Elders and Knowledge Keepers in many circles. These ceremonialists and guides have been generous role models and friends. They enlarge the circle in all that they do and create safety for people to share the important teachings that they have spent their lives learning, protecting, and honoring. These are educators of the highest degree.

It is no wonder that colonizers sought to obliterate Indigenous cultural and community ties. When your worldview holds you responsible for and in relation to all things, your connection to other beings and people—inclusive of your ancestors and the generations to come—is like a superpower. You are never alone. You are also less likely to view relations as resources, free for the taking (Cajete, 1994; Wall Kimmerer, 2013).

Put differently, a **kinship worldview** (Wahinkpe Topa & Narvaez, 2022) requires us to move from thinking that we are discrete beings separate from the natural world to being held in a web of relationships (Hart, 2002, p. 34; Little Bear, 2002, p. 79). We move from being alone and isolated to being deeply connected in relation to all things and places. Relational responsibilities go both ways; gifts and respect travel in both directions to and from our plant relatives, animal relatives, the land, the water, and the Cosmos.

I appreciate the creation story I used to read in my Montessori class, about the big bang and the universe, the earth, and eventually all things being born out of star dust. It has a beautiful synergy to the notion that our ancestors live among the stars; and in our passing, we also return to the stars as an ever-present part of the universe.

If you think about the tiny imperceptible threads that extend out from us to the more-than-human world, you feel the boundaries of self blur and stretch. You feel connections to trees, leaves, soil, and moving water, and the pheasants on the path—two male, one female—as they strut hurriedly back into the safety of the underbrush out of an evolutionary abundance of caution. Some threads may be thicker as the relational bonds feel stronger, some are whisps almost subconscious in the attachment and others feel like ropes that pull at your attention to them, depending on your relationships. Land defenders know and feel these bonds greater than anyone. The call to stand up for our water and land relatives in the face of violence. For those who do not see or feel those bonds or responsibilities, there is little understanding or empathy. Why *stand* in the way of progress?

If the threads were visible to the human eye, we could see each other in our various degrees of connection to the world. There would be those with the fewest threads walking around with the most impoverished spirits, living precariously amongst us. Others would have so many threads of relationships radiating from their bodies that it would become impossible to see the boundaries of where their skin parses their bodies from the world beyond them—the defined outline of their being blurred and the separation of themselves from the world is indistinguishable and non-existent. All the boundaries are as absolute or arbitrary as we imagine them to be.

In the moments that the connections feel most tangible, on the land, in the places I have the strongest ties and relationships, I feel the strongest, healthiest, and happiest, too. My spirit, mind, and body are nourished. I am at peace. I am inspired. I am at home.

Many people have experienced the thrill of travelling. Exploring and discovering new places. Right now, I have friends traveling in Marrakesh. They are constantly posting beautiful pictures of their experiences in the areas they are visiting. It is exciting and creates a rush for the senses, so many new things to see and take in. It can feel overwhelming and even exhausting. The relationship to place does not exist in the ways it does at home. When you are in a new place, you are meeting everything and everyone there for the first time: the air, the sounds, the sensations. The materials that make up the roads, pathways, and architecture. The land that rises from beneath your feet to greet you, anew. The plant-life that you see and breathe to share the air with is unfamiliar and unknown unless you take the time to learn who they are and what they need to live in this foreign habitat.

This ecosystem where you are the guest. In these distant places you don't have familiarity and relational knowledge that is pre-existing, established, and reciprocal. There can be a sense of danger in so much unknown.

Returning home after travel can be nourishing to your spirit in a different way. The comfort of a familiar tree in your surroundings. Winged friends that you anticipate being there. Evidence of others who co-exist in the spaces. For me, the distant sounds of river and even the highway are familiar and comforting. Seeing the distinct cuts made by beaver teeth that cause the low growing bushes to propagate additional branches in spring, that make me question the sweetness of the bark and tender growth. Is this plant a treat or a staple? Does the plant appreciate the careful pruning that instigates new cycles of growth? The beaver never overharvests; she just takes a little and moves on to the next. What lessons can be learned from observing these relationships in the places we inhabit? I know where to look in hopes of seeing a porcupine in a tree. I watch for the return of the swans that shelter safely on the far side of the frozen wetland. I know where the eagles tend to perch in the distant trees downriver. I recognize the familiar tracks of deer and jack rabbits. I linger to investigate when the paw prints are unfamiliar. Yesterday, they may have been raccoon marks near the back gate, longer claws than those of a dog, digits splayed more similarly to a human hand. *All Our Relations*.

How do we nurture our bonds and relationships with the more-than-human world (Abram, 1996)? How do we propagate new growth that will be reciprocal and mutually sustaining? I believe that place-based learning and relationships are what feed our souls and strengthen our spirits. This was not a realization that I came to overnight or with some sort of romanticized notion of learning on the land. I need to give credit to Elder Bob Cardinal of the Maskekosihk Enoch Cree Nation and Papachase scholar Dr. Dwayne Donald, and co-instructor Dr. Christine Stewart for offering the "Four Directions Teachings" course (University of Alberta, 2016). At the time of being given the place-based assignment, I was skeptical of what it could mean for me. I relied on my love of photography and reflected on my relationship with the Highwood River after the 2013 Alberta Floods (Markides, 2018, 2020a; Markides & Markides, 2020). I never imagined that would just be the beginning.

In relation to the more-than-human world, it is slow learning: relational, selfish and selfless, time spent in place. I did not know I would take the basis for that learning and carry it forward in a new place after we had moved back to the city last year, but I have. I walk out of my house, north through the neighborhood, then east towards the river, south between the Bow and the other wetland habitats, and west along the golf course road until I reach our back gate. I am in a new role, an Assistant Professor, and ceremony is a regular part of my work and personal life.

Cree scholar, Dr. Michael Hart, holds sweat lodges that create community for all who attend. I have brought my husband and my boys. My dad might also join us when his heart is feeling up for it. Anishinaabe ceremonialist Toni McCune has also become a dear friend and mentor. She has led pipe ceremonies with many of the educators and social workers I teach and in-service teacher professional learning as well. The Elders associated with the University of Calgary –Piikani Elders Reg and Rose Crowshoe, Siksika Elder Clarence Wolfleg, and Cree Métis Elder Kerrie Moore—offer prayers and lead ceremonies as part of so many campus-related events.

I am an infant in my learning from these and other Knowledge Keepers. I am surrounded by Métis and First Nations leaders in my work in the fields of education and social work. I am humbled to have these opportunities and to have this be my life. As my friend and colleague, Dr. Jennifer MacDonald, and I have often commented one of the most daunting aspects of Indigenous education is that the more you are in this learning, the more you are aware of how little you actually know (MacDonald & Markides, 2018, 2019). Depending on where people are in their journey, the reactions to my suggestions here will range widely and wildly.

As Four Arrows suggests in the Worldview Chart (Wahinkpe Topa, 2020; Wahinkpe Topa & Narvaez, 2022, pp. 5–7), the differing manifestations should not be taken as ascribing to dichotomies of absolutes, but rather along continuums of varying degrees of affinities. What we can know, connect to, understand, or believe is context specific and in flux (Little Bear, 2016, 2002). Unconsciously at first and serendipitously upon reflection, my place-study is ongoing. I am continually looking for and listening to my more-than-human relations. I seek out the bonds, and responsibilities as a thank you for the gifts these relatives bestow on me (Bouvier & MacDonald, 2019; Markides, 2020b; Wall Kimmerer, 2013). Not everyone is ready for this way of thinking, others will have always thought this way.

Reclaiming and learning these relationships is purposeful, important work. I find myself asking, how do I become a good relative for the web of relations that sustains me? In my Métis circles? In learning from Métis and First Nations teachers and ceremonialists? And in relation to the places I inhabit and co-exist with the land, water, wind, and more-than-human relatives? Pursuing the answers to these questions is a lifelong commitment. I believe that shifting to a kinship worldview is likely the only way we will be able to prevent the complete destruction of the Earth. But selfishly, it is the only way to have millions of invisible strands of relations connecting you to all aspects of the world around you. As if made by spiders, the tensile lines are infinitely stronger than they appear. The connections create physical, social, emotional, mental, and spiritual strength beyond material possessions, relationships are all that we really have in life. Becoming a good relative requires trust in the world that is outside of our control, and passion to advocate selflessly for the more-than-human beings. The place-based relationships are ever evolving, responsibilities and gifts, that we will never be isolated or alone. Interconnected and in community. Loved, valued, and accountable to being a good relative.

REFERENCES

Abram, D. (1996). *The spell of the sensuous: Perception and language in a more-than-human world.* Pantheon Books.

Absolon, K., & Willett, C. (2005). *Putting ourselves forward: Location in Aboriginal research. Research as resistance: Critical, indigenous, and anti-oppressive approaches* (pp. 97–126). Canadian Scholar's Press.

Betasamosake Simpson, L. (2014). Land as pedagogy: Nishnaabeg intelligence and rebellious transformation. *Decolonization: Indigeneity, Education & Society, 3*(3), 1–25.

Bouvier, V., & MacDonald, J. (2019). Spiritual exchange: A methodology for a living inquiry with all our relations. *International Journal of Qualitative Methods, 18,* 1–9.

Cardinal, E. B., Donald, D., & Stewart, C. (2016). *EDSE 601: Four directions teachings: A holistic inquiry in support of life and living.* University of Alberta.

Cajete, G. (1994). *Look to the mountain: An ecology of indigenous education.* Kivaki Press.

Daniels v. Canada (Indian Affairs and Northern Development). (2016). 1 S.C.R. 99, 2016 SCC12.

Hart, M. (2002). *Seeking Mino-Pimatisiwin: An Aboriginal approach to healing.* Fernwood Publishing.

King, T. (2003). *Truth about stories: A native narrative.* House of Anansi Press.

LaRocque, E. (2024). For the love of place—Not just any place: Selected Metis writings. In L. Forsythe & J. Markides (Eds.), *Around the kitchen table: Métis Aunties scholarship* (pp. 39–46). University of Manitoba Press.

Lavallee, L. (2024). Structural and lateral violence toward Metis women in the Academy. In L. Forsythe & J. Markides (Eds.), *Around the kitchen table: Métis Aunties scholarship* (pp. 136–147). University of Manitoba Press.

Little Bear, L. (2002). Jagged worldview colliding. In M. Battiste (Ed.), *Reclaiming Indigenous voice and vision* (pp. 77–85). UBC Press.

Little Bear, L. (2016). *Big thinking and rethinking: Blackfoot metaphysics 'Waiting in the Wings' [Big Thinking Lecture].* Lecture, Federation for the Humanities and Social Sciences Annual Congress, University of Calgary, Calgary, AB, Canada.

MacDonald, J., & Markides, J. (2018). Called to action: Dialogue around praxis for reconciliation. *McGill Journal of Education, 53*(2), 213–232.

MacDonald, J., & Markides, J. (2019). Duoethnography for reconciliation: Learning through conversations. *Alberta Journal of Educational Research, 65*(2), 1–16.

Markides, J. (2018). Making peace with the Highwood River: One year in contemplative photographs and flows." In P. Richardson, S. Walsh, & B. B. Artizein (Eds.), *Arts and Teaching Journal, 3*(1), 61–73.

Markides, J. (2020a). Flooded: Between two worlds, holding the memory of what used to be against the reality of what exists now. In S. Steinberg, & B. Down (Eds.), *The SAGE handbook of critical pedagogies* (pp. 604–629). Sage Publications.

Markides, J. (2020b). Overcoming (in)difference: Emancipatory pedagogy and indigenous worldviews toward respectful relationships with the more-than-human world. In J. Kirylo (Ed.), *Reinventing pedagogy of the oppressed: Contemporary critical perspectives* (pp. 157–168). Bloomsbury.

Markides, J. (2021). Examining the ethical implications and emotional entailments of teaching indigenous education: An indigenous educator's self-study. In J. Kitchen, D. Tidwell, & L. Fitzgerald (Eds.), *Self-study and diversity 3* (pp. 103–121). Brill.

Markides, J., & Markides, D. (2020). The conversation we never had: Shared autobiography in relation to place and each other. In E. Lyle (Ed.), Identity landscapes: contemplating place and the construction of self (pp. 114–123). Brill.

Shore, F. (2018). *Threads in the sash: The story of Métis people*. Pemmican Press.

St. Denis, V. (2007). Aboriginal education and anti-racist education: Building alliances across cultural and racial identity. *Canadian Journal of Education, 30*(4), 1068–1092.

University of Alberta. (2016). *EDSE 601: Four directions teachings: A holistic inquiry in support of life and living.* Elder Bob Cardinal, Dwayne Donald, and Christine Stewart.

Wahinkpe Topa (Four Arrows). (2020). *The red road (Chankyu Luta): Linking diversity and inclusion initiatives to Indigenous worldview*. Information Age Publishing.

Wahinkpe Topa (Four Arrows), & D. Narvaez. (2022). *Restoring the kinship worldview: Indigenous voices introduce 28 precepts for rebalancing life on planet earth.* North Atlantic Books.

Wall Kimmerer, R. (2013). *Braiding sweetgrass: Indigenous wisdom, scientific knowledge, and the teachings of plants.* Milkweed Editions.

Williams, K. (2021). *Stampede: Misogyny, white supremacy, and settler colonialism.* Fernwood Publishing.

CHAPTER 15

LEARNING FROM THE "LEAST OF THESE"

Haraway's "Making Kin," Filipino Indigenous "Kapwa," and Other Holistic (and Subversive) Ways of Knowing

S. Lily Mendoza

Oakland University, Rochester, MI

In this essay, I highlight cultural and communicative resources for survivance outside those in modernity, i.e., in the more-than-human agents in the natural world and in those cultures and traditions that have not (yet) severed their connection to that world. Invoking British mythologist Martin Shaw's dictum that in times of cultural crises we should seek genius not in the center, but on the edge, I argue that if we look for lessons from past cultures (and civilizations) that have undergone collapse, all the more we must strive to learn from those cultures that have been able to sustain themselves and their ways of living for millennia sans the trappings of, and dependence on, our modern industrial "civilization." In this essay, I explore Filipino Indigenous epistemologies as a way of recuperating forms of abjected knowledges and subjectivities (or ways of being) precluded in the totalizing discourse of modernity. Although Donna Haraway's notions of "making kin," "tentacular thinking," and multispecies practices of "being and becoming-with," along with new materialist understandings of object animacy and scientific discoveries affirming multispecies intelligences, are acknowledged as helpful references, the ultimate "seeing" will be grounded in the author's own tutelage to ways of knowing resonant among still land-taught Indigenous communities in her home country, the Philippines. The notion of *kapwa* (shared being or the self-in-the-other) will be explored as a radically different way of "being-with" both human and more-than-human kin in hopes of opening the canon of what counts for knowledge and communication beyond the legacy of modern Enlightenment rationality.

Keywords: Modernity, Cultural Logic, the Holy in Nature, Mari-it, Kapwa, Making Kin, Tentacular Thinking, New Materialism, Philippines, Indigenous, Survivance

INTRODUCTION: "THIS IS NOT OUR FIRST HOLOCAUST"

The key question I grapple within this study is this: In a world fast careening to the precipice of collapse, our highly technologized lifeway in the modern world continuing to wreak havoc on the Earth's ecosystems and raising questions of ultimacy having to do with the long-term viability of our invented industrial way of life, where might we look to for resources of renewal, survivance, and transformation? Note that "survivance" here, a word that has become important in Native American studies, is one first coined by Anishinaabe cultural theorist Gerald Vizenor (1999) to denote an active sense of presence, not mere survival or reaction, a way of life capable of nourishing Indigenous ways of knowing and being and ensuring their continuance and thriving.

I tackle this question as an intercultural communication scholar whose alterity – as a historically colonized, Westernized, and forcibly atomized Filipina subject – has compelled a wrestling of the issue from a place, not of shock or surprise, but of uncanny knowing, i.e., from the experience of a cultural holocaust (growing up in the aftermath of U.S.'s colonial occupation of my country for half a century) that, in my lifetime, has never not been ongoing. As Mary Louise Pratt (1994) notes ruefully, "Under conquest, social and cultural formations undergo long-term, often permanent states of crisis that cannot be resolved by either conqueror or conquered" (p. 26). The word is that we have never been here before, never before faced a calamity so planetary in scope, so catastrophic in proportion, and so far-reaching in scale and magnitude that it behooves us to wrap our heads around the likelihood of it even including our own species extinction. Everywhere we turn, the reports and predictions grow more dire each day—from the latest IPCC report in August 2021 (United Nations, 2021) issuing a virtual Code Red for human-driven global warming to countless scientific studies portentously marking the irreversible reaching of what climate scientists call "tipping points" and the triggering of "positive feedback loops" believed to radically undermine the Earth's delicate ecosystem balance.

The saying that we have never been here before may be true for us modernized humans, but for Indigenous folks all around the globe, what is going on, far from being their first holocaust, is merely an iteration of the irruption into their world of the genocidal logic of historic colonization beginning in 1492 – bringing untold destruction, suffering, and the near total annihilation of their delicately balanced lifeworld, a terror that has never really abated, but continues to be perpetrated as we speak, only now garbed in the sanitized rhetoric of "progress," "modernization," "development," "advancement," "betterment," etc.

MODERNITY: A TERRORIZING CULTURAL LOGIC

In his article "Delinking," Walter Mignolo (2007) references modernity as fomenting an "exclusionary and totalitarian notion of Totality," ("Totality" in caps in the original), i.e., "a Totality that negates, excludes, [and] occludes the difference and the possibilities of other totalities" (p. 451). Within its monopolistic oeuvre, it forecloses on the possibility of there being other ways of human *being*. As a universalized worldview, it sets up standards for who counts and who doesn't as worthwhile subjects, (re-)producing all who fail to submit to its cultural logic (of unitary coherence, rationalism, individualism, utilitarianism, and unbridled accumulation) as "misfits," "inferior beings," "primitives," "savages," etc. whose destiny is to "vanish," capitulate, or otherwise be supplanted by superior, "more evolved" human beings (Mendoza, 2019).

Today, only an estimated 350 million Indigenous Peoples remain out of a total global population of 7.8 billion, with such land-based peoples having to fight for survival and the continuance of their sacred lifeways and traditions amidst our modern culture's unrelenting assault on their territories. Interestingly, their territories are now the only remaining places in the world that have "resources" still left that can still be exploited, mined, logged, fished, and commodified. But seemingly not for long. The terror that haunts them daily is captured in the discourse of those such as the likes of former CEO of the Louisiana Pacific timber corporation, Harry Merlow, who declared proudly: "We log to infinity. Because we need it all; it's ours. It's out there, and we need it all; now… We don't log to a ten-inch top, or an eight-inch top or even a six-inch top. We log to infinity" (Chase, 1995, p. 305).

It is beyond the scope of this writing, but where my own cultural awakening (cf. Mendoza, 2005/2006) – facilitated through my encounter with the differing subjectivity and land-rooted cultures of our Indigenous Peoples in the Philippines decades ago, pulling me outside of my default bodily comportment and intellectual and communicative habituation – has led me is into a deep interrogation of the foundations and epistemological oeuvre of our now globalized system of modern industrial culture. This is one whose very condition of possibility is nothing short of the enslavement of other humans and our more-than-human kin (Nikiforuk, 2012); the domination of the natural world and its conversion into mere backdrop for the human drama which "we" deem the "real deal;" the enclosure of the commons and the invention of private ownership; the creation and normalization of violent hierarchies and standing armies; and the subjugation of all life to the logic of the market. Its singular hallmark is that of rapacious conquest, short-term profit, unbridled accumulation, supremacist ideologies, and coercive assimilation, virtually disallowing co-existence, mutuality, and collective thriving. To live by its logic without interrogation of its ontological and epistemological vision would constitute a gross analytic cataract, precluding genuine seeing and the possibility of consideration of alternative cultural visioning and imaginations of a different future.

LEARNING FROM THE "LEAST OF THESE:" CONTEMPORARY SUBVERSIONS, YES, BUT BEFORE THEN, ANCIENT WISDOM

British mythologist Martin Shaw (2016) notes that "[w]hen a culture is in crisis, genius comes not from the center, but from the edge" (n.p.). And here, I would like to argue that if we are to learn from the lessons of past cultures (and civilizations) that have undergone collapse, we must likewise learn from those cultures that have sustained themselves in place for millennia without ruining their land bases, i.e., Indigenous Peoples around the world that I refer to in this paper as—in the world's eyes—the "least of these." In my current focus on that other world that alone constitutes something other than the cultural dictates of modernity, I have noticed in the scholarly literature a beginning opening to an alternative logic emerging in the discourses of the mainstream disciplines. I note, for instance, that it is no longer just Indigenous Peoples who know that we live in a sentient, animate universe but that both scientists and humanistic thinkers themselves are discovering (belatedly) that "we are part of a living, breathing, expanding and contracting, creative and mysterious universe" (Williams, 1988, p. v) with an intelligence that demands listening and paying attention to, and that "[i]f we are to flourish," as Terry Tempest Williams (1988) argues in her Preface to eco-theologian Thomas Berry's book, *The Dream of the Earth*, "we must see ourselves as part of the journey of the universe" (p. iii).

Whether in the humanities, the social sciences, or the biological and other natural science disciplines, publications on "animate earth" (Abram, 2010), "vibrant matter" (Bennett, 2010), "plant intelligence" (Buhner, 2014), "how forests think" (Kohn, 2013), "making kin" and "tentacular thinking," (Haraway, 2016) now abound, challenging the previously dominant mechanistic models such as the notion of the natural world being nothing more than a lifeless machine, wound up like a clock, indifferent to human disposition. Across the disciplines, a rethinking of human and nature relations is giving rise to new frameworks of understanding requiring a different ethic of relation with the Earth grounded in co-thriving, reciprocity, and Earth-responsibility. Theories on the so-called "new materialism" are also now catching up and reluctantly conceding agency not just to nature beings but to the material objects that saturate our commodity world. As one publication remarked,

> This is a tectonic philosophical shift. Max Weber once described the modern era as the "progressive disenchantment of the world." A century later, a cohort of phi-

losophers of science are offering an analytic and politicized re-enchantment of the world. (Rosiek & Snyder, 2020, p. 1152)

One scholar of consequence in this regard is feminist cyborg theorist Donna Haraway, who, in her book *Cyborg Manifesto,* encourages the breaking down of boundaries between human and animal, animal-human and machine, and physical and non-physical realities. In what has become a controversial meme, "make kin, not babies," taken from a chapter in yet another one of her books, *Staying with the Trouble* (2016), she argues that it is high time that we learned "to belong in the same category with each other in such a way that has consequences" as she articulates in an interview (Paulson, 2019, n.p.) In her characteristic word-smithing inventiveness, she declares,

> We have a mammalian job to do, with our biotic and abiotic sympoietic collaborators, colaborers. We need to make kin symchthonically, sympoetically. Who and whatever we are, we need to make-with – become-with, compose-with – the earthbound. (Haraway, 2016, p. 102)

That we have failed in this kinship-making endeavor, in her estimation, is what has allowed us humans to overrun the planet, depriving our more-than-human kin of their wildlife habitat, driving their extinction rate to 1,000 times the normal. It should concern us, for example, that the pre-industrial human global population was only 1.5 billion. Today, we are counting 7.8 billion (with that number predicted to reach 11 billion by 2100). This indecent statistic, in Haraway's estimation, is also what has led to the loss of what she calls *refugia*, places of refuge that formerly allowed for the recuperation of nature and replenishment of rich cultural and biological diversity in the aftermath of such ecological decimations as desertification, soil erosion, and mass die-offs and collapse of biodiverse species populations.

But while I laud these ecologically-grounded perspectives such as that of Haraway's and other contemporary scholars, what I am even more compelled by is the fact that our Indigenous kin all over the world have long lived by these understandings for millennia that modern science is only now catching on to. Among the *katutubo,* Indigenous communities in my home country, for example, making kin is just the norm, as exemplified by the notion of *kapwa* (shared being) (Mendoza et al., 2003) or *pakikipagkapwa* (lit. "making kin-with" the other), and here, the "other" refers not only to human others but to all beings in nature. Their world is made up of a web of multispecies interrelationships where one's well-being is intricately tied to the well-being of the whole—that includes the land, the forests, the mountains, the waters, the rocks, the entire community of life. As well, there is the concept of *mari-it* (Magos, 1997; Nalangan, 2018), places in the Wild watched over by *taglugar,* (spirit guardians) and understood as off-limits to humans. Such spirit guardians (invariably known as *engkanto*) are believed to be the owners of the earth. Hence, "[h]umans must first ask their permission before cutting down their tree abodes, burning their mountains, or destroying their anthills" (Meñez, 1996, p. 64). For millennia, it is what has taught people to respect boundaries deemed to have been drawn by the Holy Wild herself, transgression of which has been known to lead to dire consequences such as physical illness, insanity, or even death.

This is now what I find myself being drawn to more and more in my work—the radicality of what the differing ethic of Indigenous life has to offer amidst the chaos spawned in our world by modern hubris, one signified by a sacredness of relation with living Earth and maintained through a ritual way of being—the observance of protocols of courtesy, asking for permission, and communicative expressions of utmost subtlety, beauty, and eloquence. Their chanting, ornate mythic storytelling, dancing, beautiful grieving, etc.—ceremonially performed—understood to be the language taught to them by the Holy in Nature herself. Not taking anything without giving something back puts constraints on human acquisitiveness. And in this cosmological worldview, humans don't reign supreme; Nature does. But, like all other beings, humans as well have their important part to play in keeping Life alive. As I noted in an essay reflecting on my first-hand encounters with some of our Indigenous communities:

> I have glimpsed life-giving beauty—the building of a Manobo *tinandasan* hut using no nails, with each piece of bamboo, nipa, or rattan, sang to and praised before harvest until permission is granted; master builders still retaining memory of the old way of doing things; a people who co-exist and honor the crocodiles on their marshlands as the Spirit Guardians of the waters (in stark contrast to the town Mayor's bloodlust upon capturing—and eventually killing—the crocodile Lolong, touted as the largest in the world); a woman Indigenous leader being ministered to in ceremony by Muslim *patutunong* healers so she could finally accept her calling to become a healer herself; native youth taking up the mantle of leadership in fighting corporate encroachment of their ancestral lands; the laughter of *Manangs* and *Manongs* as they told their stories, and the beautiful chanting of other elders in response.
>
> It is these kinds of encounters—with our Indigenous Peoples and those working on the ground alongside them—that now serves as the homeward beacon for me. Just like native peoples everywhere else around the globe threatened by the relentless incursion of our extractive economy into their territories, our own Indigenous kin in the Philippine homeland struggle bravely to keep their beautiful ways of being alive amidst the assault. The grief (at their beleaguered condition) compels, but so does the grace, beauty, and courage of their spirit. (Mendoza, 2020, pp. 60–61)

As for the theoretical implications of this way of being for re-imagining how we in our field (intercultural communication) might do our work differently, I can only reference a piece I wrote recently (Mendoza, forthcoming) titled, "Theorizing at the End of the World: Transforming Critical Intercultural Communication," which I ended with the following closing passage (and with this, I will end):

The archive opened up here (providing a glimpse of modernity's ultimate "other") [i.e., the Indigenous] presents a mirror, an alternative cultural logic of connection, cooperation, community, reciprocity, mutual thriving, and the embrace of limits that can guide us on a way forward. To point to its significance, I take inspiration from the words of Indian writer, Arundhati Roy (2012):

The first step towards reimagining a world gone terribly wrong would be to stop the annihilation of those who have a different imagination . . . an imagination which has an altogether different understanding of what constitutes happiness and fulfillment . . . *who may look like the keepers of our past but who may really be the guides to our future.* (p. 214, emphasis added)

REFERENCES

Abram, D. (2010). *Becoming animal: An earthly cosmology.* Vintage Books.
Bennett, J. (2010). *Vibrant matter: A political ecology of things.* Duke University Press.
Buhner, S. H. (2014). *Plant intelligence and the imaginal realm: Beyond the doors of perception into the dreaming of earth.* Bear & Company Books.
Chase, A. (1995). *In a dark wood: The fight over forests and the rising tyranny of ecology.* Houghton Mifflin Harcourt Publishing Company.
Haraway, D. J. (2016). *Staying with the trouble: Making kin in the Chthulucene.* Duke University Press.
Kohn, E. (2013). *How forests think: Toward an anthropology beyond the human.* University of California Press.
Magos, A. P. (1997). *The concept of Mari-it (Dangerous Zones) in panaynon worldview and its impact on sustainable human development.* SEAMEO-Jasper Fellowship Monograph Series 5.
Mendoza, S. L. (2024). Theorizing at the end of the world: Transforming critical intercultural communication. In T. K. Nakayama & R. T. Halualani (Eds.), *The handbook of critical intercultural communication* (Revised Edition, pp. 109–126). Blackwell Publishing.
Mendoza, S. L. (2005)/(2006). Tears in the archive: Creating memory to survive and contest empire. In M. W. Lustig & J. Koester (Eds.), *Among US: Essays on identity, belonging, and intercultural competence* (pp. 233–245, Rev. ed.). Pearson.
Mendoza, S. L. (2019). Promises of the 'Vanishing' Worlds: Re-Storying 'Civilization' in the Philippine National Imaginary. *Canadian Journal of Native Studies, XXXIX*(1), 119–143.
Mendoza, S. L. (2020). Hope summons: Meditations on an-other-world seeing. *ReVision, 33*(3), 15–24.
Mendoza, S. Perkinson, L., & Perkinson, J. (2003). Filipino 'Kapwa' in Global Dialogue: A Different Politics of Being-With the 'Other.' *Intercultural Communication Studies, 12*(4), 177–193.
Meñez, H. Q. (1996). *Explorations in Philippine folklore.* Ateneo de Manila Press.
Mignolo, W. D. (2007). Delinking. *Cultural Studies, 21*(2), 449–514.
Nalangan, A. R. I. (2018). *The Mari-it in twelve selected folktales of Malay, Aklan.* Undergraduate Thesis, University of the Philippines Visayas.
Nikiforuk, A. (2012). *The energy of slaves: Oil and the new servitude.* Greystone Books.

Paulson, S. (2019). *Making kin: An interview with Donna Haraway.* LA Review of Books. December 6, 2019. https://lareviewofbooks.org/article/making-kin-an-interview-with-donna-haraway/.

Pratt, M. L. (1994). Transculturation and autoethnography: Peru1615/1980. In F. Barker, P. Hulme, & M. Iversen (Eds.), *Colonial discourse/Postcolonial theory* (pp. 24–46). Manchester University Press..

Rosiek, J. L., & Snyder, J. (2020). Narrative inquiry and new materialism: Stories as (Not necessarily benign) agents. *Qualitative Inquiry*, 26(10), 1151–1162. https://doi.org/10.1177/1077800418784326.

Roy, A. (2012). *Walking with the comrades.* Penguin Book.

Shaw, M. (2016). *Trailing the gods back home: An interview with Dr. Martin Shaw.* https://www.youtube.com/watch?v=g28G7GOym_I Last accessed: June 19, 2021.

United Nations. (2021). *IPCC report: 'Code red' for human driven global heating, warns UN chief.* August 9, 2021. https://news.un.org/en/story/2021/08/1097362#:~:text=The%20report%20explains%20that%20from,in%20other%20greenhouse%20gas%20emissions.

Vizenor, G. (1999). *Manifest manners: Narratives on postindian survivance.* University of Nebraska Press.

Williams, T. T. (1988). Preface. In Thomas Berry (Ed.), *The dream of the earth* (pp. i-vi). Sierra Club Books.

BOOK REVIEW

INDIGENOUS WISDOM FOR RESTORING OUR WORLD

Vicki Zakrzewski

University of California, Berkeley, Berkeley, CA

A review of the important recent book by the Editor of this volume, Wahinkpe Topa (Four Arrows).

Keywords: Sacred Feminine, Spiritual Perspective, Interconnectedness, Indigenous Voices, Climate Change

Indigenous Wisdom for Restoring Our World: A Book Review of *Restoring a Kinship Worldview: Indigenous Voices Introduce 28 Precepts for Rebalancing on Planet Earth*.

The human race needs a reset. When considering the incredibly complex challenges facing us today—climate change, racism, inequality, isolation, among others—at the root of every single one of them is a value-system choice. But to make real change, we need to dig even deeper than our values and get to our beliefs and ensuing assumptions. Because ultimately, it is those beliefs and assumptions—or "worldview"—that drive our actions and choices.

Four Arrows and Darcia Narvaez's book *Restoring a Kinship Worldview: Indigenous Voices Introduce 28 Precepts for Rebalancing on Planet Earth* offers readers the opportunity to deeply examine their own worldview, covering a variety of elemental topics such as community welfare, generosity and gift-giving, economics, nature, death and dying, and time. They argue that only two worldviews exist: one that sees Nature as "intelligent and living" (the Kinship worldview) and one that essentially does not (the Eurocentric worldview). This seemingly simple dichotomy has profound implications for the health and well-being of people and our ecosystem, depending on which worldview dominates. When humans are centered in a Kinship worldview—one grounded in the "common precepts shared by Indigenous peoples" (Four Arrows & Narvaez, 2022, p. 3) around the world—the focus is on interconnectedness, the innate goodness of humans, and "courage and fearless trust in the universe" (Four Arrows & Narvaez, 2022, p. 33) In contrast, the Eurocentric worldview promotes an anthropocentric view of life, resulting in a society that champions personal gain, materialism, and hierarchy.

To illustrate their argument, the authors include a chart in the "Introduction" that provides a comparative list of how the two worldviews manifest. For instance, the common dominant worldview shows up as "emphasis on rights," "social laws of society are primary," and "conflict resolution with revenge, punishment." In contrast, the Indigenous worldview indicates "emphasis on responsibility," "laws of Nature are primary," and "conflict resolution as return to community" (Four Arrows, 2020 quoted in Four Arrows & Narvaez, 2022, p. 6). But the authors are quick to point out that each item on the list should be viewed as a continuum, offering readers who lean towards a Eurocentric worldview a guide for self-examination of their own beliefs and assumptions—and the opportunity to consider another way of being in the world.

The organization of the book is unique: each chapter begins with an excerpt by a member of an Indigenous group, setting the stage for the exploration of a topic that is foundational to how we operate in the world, but that may lie unexamined because it falls beneath the surface of our conscious mind—a notorious minefield of behavior-driven assumptions. The excerpt is then followed by a dialogue between the authors that explains in greater detail the meaning and implications of the selection, supported by the authors' own experiences, research, and personal views.

For instance, a chapter on community welfare opens with a passage from Doña Enriqueta Contreras, a Zapotecan healer, midwife, and teacher, known for her work in applying the "wisdom of curanderismo (folk healing)." She outlines the Zapotecan principles that form the basis of caring for the community: to know that "everything has life," to hold reverence for Nature and our ancestors, and to recognize our relationship with Mother Nature—a set of beliefs that are in contradistinction to a worldview that believes in the domination of Nature and that is frighteningly out of touch when it comes to caring for others. In the dialogue that follows, the authors offer examples that beautifully illustrate the dire need for the kind of care that recognizes our interdependence with Nature and with each other. In a heart-wrenching example, Narvaez discusses two films that share a message from the Kogi priests (Mamas) of South America who sensed the "weakening of the earth," urging humans to change their harmful practices. To show viewers the intersection of Indigenous knowledge with science, the filmmakers consulted scientists who confirmed that research does, in fact, support the Kogi knowledge of climate. (In a similar fashion throughout the book, the authors include many examples of science that validate ancient Indigenous wisdom.)

Four Arrows brings care of the community to a more micro-level, focusing on the importance of listening to one another—but listening in such a way that involves "seeking a spiritual perspective." Indeed, he describes witnessing elders "find a sacred place on the earth or gaze at a star, as if to get help in understanding what is being communicated." In a delightful story that illustrates this deep form of listening, Four Arrows shares an experience in which children came to the rescue of a group of Indigenous leaders. After watching their elders angrily disagree on an issue, the children quietly left the room for a while, then returned to ask the elders to join them outside. As each child shared their thoughts, Four Arrows found himself listening "in the old Indigenous ways," helping him to recall the greater purpose of their work—one that is grounded in humility, respect, and interdependence.

And yet, this kind of care for the community is difficult to achieve if we ourselves do not feel cared for—an argument that Narvaez returns to throughout the book in an effort to urge readers to examine and question the unnatural ways in which western societies raise their children. In a chapter on respecting the sacred feminine, she points to the research that shows how parenting practices that distress babies result in psychological illnesses such as emotional dysregulation and the inability to foster healthy, egalitarian relationships, ultimately creating a society that is filled with "impaired adults" who continue the cycle of "undercare." Instead, children need what Narvaez calls the "evolved nest," or ancient nurturing practices, such as community support in which both the mother and the child feel welcome, continuous carrying or holding of the baby, and quick responses to a child's needs. Experiencing this kind of care early on helps us to develop a moral compass grounded in compassion rather than self-protection. In other words, we move away from the Eurocentric worldview that fosters selfishness and greed resulting from a deep sense of insecurity and towards the kinship worldview of sharing and abundance, grounded in interdependence.

The richness of the content and depth of wisdom contained in this book cannot be justly captured in a short review that only scratches the surface. But perhaps it can be summed up in a striking quote from Lakota member Martin Brokenleg and co-authors that opens one of the chapters: "The highest expression of courage is generosity" (Brendtro et al., 2019 quoted in Four Arrows & Narvaez 2022, 148). Contained within this seed of an idea is perhaps the essence of the Kinship worldview: To be generous towards another human being and towards Nature means that we are grounded in a "fearless trust" of an abundant and benevolent Universe of which we and all others are a significant part, deserving of respect, dignity, compassion, gratitude, love, and healing.

This book offers hope in the face of seemingly intractable problems created by the currently dominant worldview. I recommend that you read this book slowly, savor it, and ponder the new "old" way of being in the world that it offers. Imagine how it might feel to live fearlessly in a sentient world, connected and cared for, prioritizing a relational rather than a material consciousness. Take up the invitation proffered by Oneida-Mohawk-Cree comedian Charlie Hill: "Come to us now. We can fix this country. All the problems it has. We can fix it because we have the owner's manual" (Hill 2019 as quoted in Four Arrows & Narvaez 2022, p. 166).

REFERENCES

Brendtro, L., Brokenleg, M., & Van Bockern, S. (2019). *Reclaiming youth at risk: Our hope for the future* (3rd ed.). Solution Tree Press.

Four Arrows. (2020). *The red road (chanku luta): Linking diversity and inclusion initiatives to indigenous worldview.* Information Age Publishing.

Four Arrows, & Narvaez, D. (2022). *Restoring the kinship worldview: Indigenous voices introduce 28 precepts for rebalancing life on planet earth.* North Atlantic Books.

Hill, C. (2019). *American Indian Comedy Slam: Goin Native No Reservations Needed.* Directed by Scott Montoya. Laugh Out Loud Comedy Inc., aired December 2009 on Showtime, filmed during the Laugh Out Loud Comedy Festival. Quoted in Laugh Out Loud Flix, "Charlie Hill: Remembering a Native American Comedy Legend." October 14, 2019. Video, 12:21. www.youtube.com/watch?v=RaWTGnA9xrY.

BIOGRAPHIES

Art Blume is an American Indian scholar and Professor at Washington State University. He served as president of the Society of Indian Psychologists in 2015–2017. He has been honored with the Trimble and Horvat Award for Distinguished Contributions to Native and Indigenous Psychology, a Rockefeller Foundation Fellowship, and as President's Professor, University of Alaska Fairbanks Center for Alaska Native Health Research. Published extensively in multicultural psychology, his book, *A new psychology based on community, equality, and care of the Earth: An Indigenous American perspective*, was awarded a 2021 American Library Association Choice Award for Outstanding Academic Title.

Frank Bracho is a Venezuelan of Arawak heritage. A passionate Indigenous activist, he is author of numerous books on health, the environment and economics. He was once Venezuela's ambassador to India and has advised several presidents of Venezuela. He is currently organizing an international Indigenous People's conference to be held in a natural biodiversity-rich country such as Colombia that will express the urgency for bringing Indigenous leadership to the fore before it is too late.

Kinship Worldview: Indigenous Authors Going
Deeper with Holistic Education, pages 101–105.
Copyright © 2024 by Information Age Publishing
www.infoagepub.com
All rights of reproduction in any form reserved.

BIOGRAPHIES

Gregory Cajete is a Tewa Indian from Santa Clara Pueblo, New Mexico. He has lectured at colleges and universities around the world. He served as Dean of the Center for Research and Cultural Exchange, the Institute of American Indian Arts, and Director of Native American Studies and an emeritus Professor in the Division of Language, Literacy and Socio-cultural Studies in the College of Education at the University of New Mexico. He has authored 10 books, including *Look to the Mountain: An Ecology of Indigenous Education; Native Science: Natural Laws of Interdependence and Critical Neurophilosophy and Indigenous Wisdom* (co-authored with Four Arrows and Jongmin Lee), and *Sacred Journeys: Personal Visions of Indigenous Education* (John Charlton Publishers Ltd.). Dr. Cajete also has written chapters in 37 other books along with numerous articles and has given over 300 national and international presentations.

Paul Freedman is the founding Head of School at Salmonberry School in Eastsound, WA. He is Senior Editor of *Holistic Education Review*. He serves on the faculty of The Institute for Educational Studies (TIES). He is currently pursuing his EdD at Fielding Graduate University, where his research interests are in the area of international holistic school leadership. Paul has published numerous articles and presented at many conferences in the field of holistic education. He is the father of two amazing young adults and lives with his wife, Andria and a menagerie of farm animals on Orcas Island in the Salish Sea.

Brett Grant, Ph.D., is a postdoctoral researcher with the Black Education Research Center (BERC) at Teachers College, Columbia University, and a Community Faculty member at Metropolitan State University in Saint Paul, Minnesota. Dr. Grant is currently the co-program chair for the Holistic Education Special Interest Group for the American Education Research Association.

Miranda Haskie is a Professor of Sociology at Diné College in Tsaile, AZ. She is co-author of The Future of Navajo Education.

Wahinkpe Topa (Four Arrows), aka Don Trent Jacobs, is an Oglala Lakota Pipe Carrier, made a relative through one of the Lakota's seven sacred ceremonies, *Huŋkápi* after completing his Sun Dance vows on Pine Ridge with Rick Two Dogs. Formerly Director of Education at Oglala Lakota College, he is currently a professor with Fielding Graduate University in the School of Leadership Studies. He has authored numerous books, chapters, papers and articles on Indigenous worldview and counter-hegemonic education. Recipient of the Martin Springer Institutes Moral Courage Award for his activism, his most recent co-authored book, *Restoring the Kinship Worldview: 28 Indigenous Voices Introduce Worldview Precepts for Rebalancing Life on Planet Earth* was selected by UC Berkeley's Science Center for the Greater Good as one of the top 15 "thought provoking, inspiring and practical" science books of 2022. He lives in Mexico and in Canada with his artist wife and numerous pets.

Shannon Kenny, social entrepreneur and published author. She began her career as a historian and has worked as a freelance writer, editor, and educator in the fields of history, social sciences, and social justice for over 20 years. In 2018, Shannon founded technology startup Prontopia (Alliloop.io), to solve workforce supply gaps in caregiving jobs. Informed by the Indigenous women's leadership activism of her mother, Carolyn Kenny, Shannon's work seeks to restore balance to the interplay of technology and society by recognizing where technology companies have forsaken human connection to each other and to the land for short-term gains focused on minimizing human effort.

Lone Wolf was born in Pine Ridge in 1953 to Flora Curry (Glenn) and Albert Curry Sr. She was orphaned when I was 11 months old when my mother was killed in a car accident. She attended boarding schools thereafter. In 1984 she became a counselor at Oglala Lakota College. Continuing her education, she became a faculty member and Vice-President for Instruction. She currently is OLC's coordinator for the American Indian Higher Education Consortium and a Student senate advisor. Ms. Lone Wolf was born in Pine Ridge in 1953 to Flora Curry (Glenn) and Albert Curry Sr. She was orphaned at 11 months when her mother was killed in a car accident. She attended boarding schools thereafter. In 1984 she became a counselor at Oglala Lakota College. Continuing her education, she became a faculty member and Vice-President for Instruction. She currently is a faculty member at Oglala Lakota College in the Social Work Department. Devona has been at the college since 1984.

Jennifer Markides is a SSHRC Tier II Canada Research Chair in Indigenous Youth Well-Being and Education, and an Assistant Professor in the Werklund School of Education and the Faculty of Social Work at the University of Calgary, Canada. She is a member of the Métis Nation of Alberta with family ties originating in Red River and extending across the homeland. Her research is community-driven and prioritizes the goals and interests of Indigenous youth, their families, and communities, inclusive of language revitalization, cultural teachings, and holistic wellbeing.

S. Lily Mendoza is a Professor of Culture and Communication at Oakland University. She hails from the Philippines, growing up in the traditional homelands of the Ayta Peoples. She is known for her scholarship on the problematic logic of modernity and the complex politics of Indigeneity. She is also the Executive Director of the non-profit Center for Babaylan Studies (CfBS), a movement for decolonization and Indigenization among diasporic Filipinos in North America and beyond.

Ilarion (Kuuyux) Merculieff is Unangan (Aleut). His people have survived and thrived for over 10,000 years in the Bering Sea and they are still there. Ilarion was given his traditional name of Kuuyux at age 4. Kuuyux means an arm extending out from the body, a carrier of ancient knowledge to modern times, a messenger. He is now living the legacy of his name.

Amba J. Sepie is a transdisciplinary author, teacher and creative collaborator working in the fields of decolonization, culture repair and soul medicine. She is currently a Whitinga Science Fellow and researcher based at Massey University in Aotearoa New Zealand.

Sox Sperry is the founder and curator of provensustainable.org. His vocation has been to design and implement structures by which small groups can work collectively to deepen awareness of the role of the individual in family and community. He began his teaching career at the Learning Center, a parent teacher cooperative elementary school in Fort Wayne, Indiana. He went on to co-found the Center for Nonviolence in Fort Wayne where he facilitated nonviolence education classes for adult and teen men. Since 2007 Sox has worked as primary curriculum writer with Project Look Sharp, a media literacy integration initiative at Ithaca College.

Deepa Srikantaiah, Ph.D., is an educator, artist, and researcher. Dr. Srikantaiah's research interests focus on pre-colonial knowledge systems and Indigenous Knowledges, contemplative studies, and mathematics and science education. She is currently an affiliate faculty in the International Education Policy Program in the College of Education at the University of Maryland, College Park, and for the Ed.D. program at the School for International Training. She also adjuncts in the Urban Teachers Program at American University, Washington, D.C. Dr. Srikantaiah is currently the program chair for the Holistic Education Special Interest Group for the American Education Research Association.

Ethleen Iron Cloud Two Dogs is of the Knife Chief Buffalo Nation that takes care of a herd of buffalo used for sustenance and spiritual purposes. She is the wife of the highly respected spiritual leader and interpreter of the sacred for the Oglala Lakota Sioux. Ethleen is a Program Director for the Mental Health Project in the Oglala Sioux Tribe in South Dakota. As a member of the Ethnicity, Race and Mental Health Commission and a leader of the Oglala Women's Equity Movement, her presentations appear a number of times in C-SPAN Library, with her first appearance in 2002.

Shytance Wren, M. A, is a second-year doctoral student studying International Education Policy in the College of Education at the University of Maryland, College Park. In her research, she addresses critical issues surrounding globalization, knowledge production, and policy borrowing in higher education. Currently, she is examining college and university transformational practices that ensure success for Black, Latino, and Indigenous students, as well as students from low-income backgrounds.

Tyson Yunkaporta is an Aboriginal scholar, founder of the Indigenous Knowledge Systems Lab at Deakin University in Melbourne, and author of *Sand Talk*. His work focuses on applying Indigenous methods of inquiry to resolve complex issues and explore global crises.

Vicki Zakrzewski is the founding Education Director at the Greater Good Science Center at the University of California, Berkeley, where she translates the science of compassion, empathy, gratitude, awe, forgiveness, and other social, emotional, and ethical skills to improve the well-being of students and educators. She has partnered with numerous organizations such as UNESCO, CASEL, the Mind and Life Institute (of which she is a fellow), Harvard's Making Caring Common and EASEL Lab, the Jim Henson Company, and Pixar/Disney. She is the creative lead for the free online resource for educators Greater Good in Education and the co-associate editor of practice for the journal *Social and Emotional Learning: Research, Practice, and Policy*.

www.ingramcontent.com/pod-product-compliance
Lightning Source LLC
Chambersburg PA
CBHW070631300426
44113CB00010B/1730